FISHING TANDEM FLIES

FISHING TANDEM FLIES

Tactics, Techniques, and Rigs to Catch More Trout

Charles Meck

Illustrations by Dave Hall

*Headwater
Books*

To my brother, Gerald (Jerry) Meck, of Massillon, Ohio.
Although he was the older brother, he always had time for me.
We traveled to many destinations in search of trout.
Jerry bravely fought cancer for more than 14 years, and during
that long battle, he had a truly positive outlook on life.
He will be deeply missed and never forgotten.
May he rest in peace.

Copyright © 2007 by Charles Meck

Published by
HEADWATER BOOKS
531 Harding Street
New Cumberland, PA 17070
www.headwaterbooks.com

Printed in U.S.A.

First edition

10 9 8 7 6 5 4 3 2 1

ISBN: 978-0-9793460-0-2

Cover design by Caroline Stover and David Siegfried
Cover photograph by Jay Nichols

Library of Congress Control Number: 2007930345

CONTENTS

CHAPTER 1

Double Vision

Dave Trimble was dogged by one annoying problem. Dave is a guide—a great guide—on the Lee's Ferry section of the Colorado River in northern Arizona. Gary Hitterman, Howard Nixon, and I hired Dave for a day, and on the ride upriver to Marble Canyon Dam, I made some small talk with Dave and asked about the largest trout he had caught on the river. Last year, he said, he landed an 18-inch rainbow, but he was a little embarrassed he hadn't caught one bigger. I could see that my question bothered him. Dave explained that part of his problem was that he guided clients almost every day and had few days off to fish.

Gary, Howard, and I fished for the first few hours, and we caught plenty of rainbows, but nothing larger than 18 inches. I caught more than a dozen trout on a blue beadhead Glo Bug that I call the Blueberry. At about 10 A.M. I walked over to Dave and handed him my rod so that he could fish. I let him use the rig that was working for me, which was a Blueberry fished under a Looped-Leader Patriot. Dave hadn't seen a looped-leader fly before and was intrigued.

Dave saw some large rainbows finning in shallow water twenty feet off the bank. We set the distance between the dry fly and the wet at three feet so the Blueberry would drift near the bottom. Dave slowly waded to within casting range. His casting was on the mark, and he fished the pair of flies flawlessly: the highly visible dry fly

1

Dave Trimble hoists a goliath Lee's Ferry rainbow caught on a tandem rig.

floated drag-free on the surface while the weighted Blueberry drifted near the bottom. His first cast, nothing. His second, no strike. His third drift, still no hookup. On his fourth cast, a fish took the Blueberry, the Patriot promptly sank, and Dave set the hook. A goliath rainbow headed downriver, closely followed by Dave. I ran after him with an oversized net. After twenty minutes, Dave landed the 24-inch beauty, and before releasing it, held the fish triumphantly toward the sky, thanking the fishing gods.

"Now you can tell all of your clients that you caught a 24-incher," I said, sharing in Dave's pride as he measured the rainbow.

"I did it," Dave bellowed, his happy voice echoing up and down the canyon walls. The Blueberry worked again!

I first used the tandem rig in 1984 on central Oregon's McKenzie River with guide Ken Helfrich. Mike Manfredo and I were there to fish the March Brown hatch, which provides great fishing on that river in early April. Ken tied a size 12 Western March Brown dry fly on a 24-inch dropper and tied a dark-brown wet fly to the tippet. When I cast that rig, my flies twisted into bird's-nest tangles, and I didn't pursue fishing with two flies.

But my opinion of fishing tandem flies later changed. In 1> to complete the research for *Great Rivers, Great Hatches*, I fished more than forty rivers across the United States with twenty different guides. I learned a lot from each of them. One taught me the finer elements of high-stick nymphing. Another taught me how to fish a bouquet during a Trico spinner fall. (A bouquet is three to five Trico spinners tied on a large hook like a size 14 or 16. To a feeding trout it looks like a cluster of several spinners.) My guide on Oregon's Deschutes introduced me to the pleasure of salsa served onstream. That year I purchased nineteen nonresident fishing licenses, and I fished streams and rivers from Pennsylvania to Washington.

It was August 18, and coauthor Greg Hoover and I had a September 1 deadline for our manuscript. My son, Bryan, and I fished for the past week on many of Montana's finest rivers. But, the fishing wasn't going well. Phil Baldachino of Kettle Creek Outfitters in Pennsylvania suggested that we hire Richie Montella to guide us on the Big Horn River in southwestern Montana. I contacted Richie, and he agreed to guide us for two days. Well, our frustration continued that first morning. Few trout rose and even fewer hit my dry fly. Richie saw the disappointment in our faces. After about two hours of going fishless, he asked us to fish a wet fly behind our dry fly.

Richie connected the flies differently than Helfrich. He tied on a size 12 easy-to-see white-winged dry fly and connected a size 12 Beadhead Pheasant Tail on 36 inches of tippet to that hook's bend with an improved clinch. In a short time, I learned to cast the two flies slower and open my loop a little more. By my tenth cast, my luck changed. The dry fly sank; I set the hook and landed a heavy brown on the nymph. That was simple enough. I made a few more casts, the dry fly sank again, and I hooked another big brown. Several more casts and another brown took the nymph. Bryan mirrored my success.

If we didn't fish nymphs this way, the day would have been a bust. I became an advocate of the tandem. In fact, fishing tandem flies forever changed the way I fished. After our success on the Big Horn, I tried the tandem back East, and it worked just as well. For that matter, fishing tandem flies has saved me from frustrating trips on trout water around the country.

After two decades of fishing almost exclusively with two or more flies, I have refined the system to make it even easier. In this book, I hope to help you become more prepared to meet some of the onstream challenges that we all love about fly fishing. In chapters 2 through 7, I'll share some tactics and techniques I've learned and developed over the years for fishing tandem rigs, including tactics for matching the hatch and how to rig the different connections, and in chapters 8 and 9, I'll share some effective flies I've discovered over the years. These methods might change the way you fish.

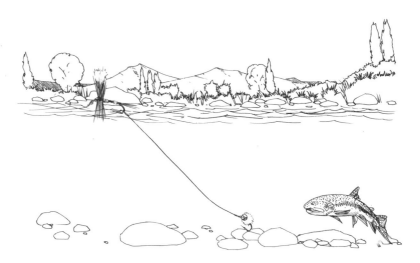

A Beadhead Glo Bug fished under a Patriot is one of my favorite combinations when nothing is hatching. Trout can't resist egg patterns.

CHAPTER 2

Tandem Flies

If you're as old as me, then you remember how good fishing was back in the mid-1940s—trout were plentiful and fly fishers were few, making for much better odds. I rarely met another fly caster in an entire day of fishing. Back then, wet flies were sold with six inches of heavy cat-gut leader snelled to the hook eye with a loop on the other end. By attaching that loop to a loop on the leader with a loop-to-loop connection, we fished two, three, or even four wet flies at once and easily changed flies to find the right combination that worked. I often cast a brace of wet flies across or three-quarters downstream and twitched them as they made their turn to imitate the way a lot of insects emerge. It was a deadly way to fish.

That method has, for the most part, disappeared. Occasionally I'll hear from an old-timer who still fishes that way, but nowadays, when most anglers fish more than one fly at a time, they suspend one or more nymphs under a high-floating dry fly or strike indicator. Rather than swing the flies, modern tandem aficionados often fish the two patterns drag-free, floating naturally with the current. Most of us don't fish the classic wets anymore; instead, we fish nymphs, a generic term for the wide range of subsurface patterns ranging from caddis and midge larvae and pupae to mayfly nymphs and emergers to sunken terrestrials and submerged spinners. However,

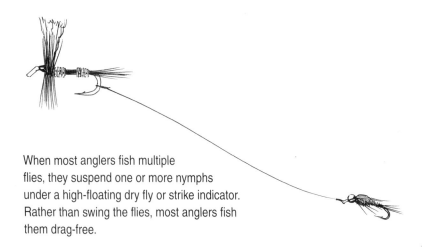

When most anglers fish multiple flies, they suspend one or more nymphs under a high-floating dry fly or strike indicator. Rather than swing the flies, most anglers fish them drag-free.

many wise anglers have not forgotten that those old wets caught plenty of fish, and they are making a comeback, especially soft-hackles.

Fishing a combination of dry flies and nymphs or more than one subsurface pattern—also called a tandem rig—is one of the simplest, most effective ways to fish. It has become increasingly popular on trout waters across the country. When I talk about tandem flies in this book, I mean two or more flies fished at the same time. Those flies could be one dry and one wet, one dry and two wets, two dry flies, two wets, three wets, and even more combinations. This book is about the combinations, how to connect and fish them, and what patterns I like to use.

For more than forty years I fished dry flies almost exclusively because they were easy to follow and the action occurred on the surface where I could see it. Wet flies, on the other hand, always frustrated me. I knew that day in and day out wet flies caught more trout, but I had difficulty detecting strikes.

A lot of skilled fly fishers intensely watch the end of their fly lines, or strike indicators, waiting for the first indication of a strike so they can quickly set the hook. I can't bear this for long. With a tandem rig, I could watch a dry fly, which for me is a more exciting and interesting way to fish a nymph. Also, the fortuitous strikes on the dry fly that I would never have had give me great delight.

One benefit of fishing a dry fly instead of a conventional strike indicator is that you often hook fish on the dry when you least expect to. This brook trout took the oversized indicator fly aggressively.

Because I love to watch a dry fly drift and bob along in the currents, my favorite versions of the tandem rig are ones with dry flies. I either fish a looped-leader dry fly as a dropper while the nymph dangles below on point or fish a nymph tied on to the bend of a dry-fly indicator, the most common form of fishing tandem flies in the United States (in this connection, the nymph is commonly referred to as the dropper). In both types of the rigs, the dry fly, usually brightly colored and easy to see, acts as both a strike indicator and a second floating fly. Tied to tippet connected either directly to the dry fly or to the leader below the dry fly, a nymph or emerger drifts below the surface at a depth determined by the length of tippet you use. While I typically only fish one subsurface fly beneath the floating indicator fly, you can easily fish two subsurface flies as long as you adjust your casting technique and use a dry fly that has the right characteristics to float both flies. Even though I most frequently use a dry fly and a nymph, you can use two or more dry flies or two or more wets, depending on your fishing preferences or the problems you are trying to solve.

Tandem rigs aren't just for trout. This Great Lakes steelhead took a bright pink Copper John, which was tied to the bend of an egg pattern.

Tandem rigs aren't just for trout—Great Lakes steelhead anglers have long used bright chartreuse Glo Bugs or white Zonkers to attract fish to their second fly (and to help them track their rig so that they can strike when the fish opens its mouth) and some bass anglers trail a streamer behind a popper fished on the surface. The splashy popper draws the fish's attention to the streamer.

TERMINOLOGY

We inherited many of the terms for fishing tandem flies from England, where anglers have fished a series of wet flies, called a cast, for hundreds of years. The traditional cast has two or more droppers (flies tied to leader) and a point fly (the last fly tied to the tippet). Droppers are connected to the leader in a variety of ways and most often come off the leader at right angles. The final fly in the rig, attached directly to the tippet, is called the point.

When we add a dry fly to the rig—more specifically, when we tie a piece of tippet to the eye or the bend (the most popular) of a dry fly—we call the second fly attached to the dry fly the dropper. You'll often hear a dry fly and a nymph referred to as a dry-and-dropper rig. As a general rule, anything added to a fly tied to the tippet can be called a dropper. This broad definition covers both droppers tied to the leader before the final fly and a nymph or other dry fly tied to the bend of a primary dry fly.

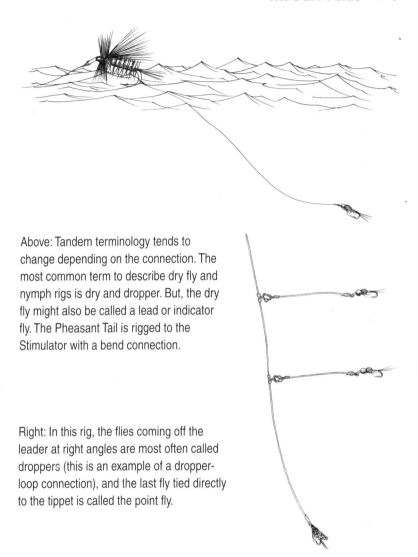

Above: Tandem terminology tends to change depending on the connection. The most common term to describe dry fly and nymph rigs is dry and dropper. But, the dry fly might also be called a lead or indicator fly. The Pheasant Tail is rigged to the Stimulator with a bend connection.

Right: In this rig, the flies coming off the leader at right angles are most often called droppers (this is an example of a dropper-loop connection), and the last fly tied directly to the tippet is called the point fly.

The terminology I use tends to change with the connection. In traditional wet-fly rigs, I call the fly attached directly to the tippet, the point fly, and the flies attached to the leader, droppers. When referring to fly combinations that include a dry fly, I often use the terms dry and dropper, indicator fly and terminal fly, or first and last fly. Sometimes I refer to the first fly in the series as the lead fly.

CONNECTIONS

In this book, I cover the following seven connections: bend, dropper, dropper loop, two eye, tag, looped leader, and movable dropper. They all have pros and cons, and I favor some over others, but knowing how to rig all of them might give you some creative and effective ideas for catching more fish.

Bend

Connecting flies in-line by the bends of the hooks is probably the most versatile and effective way of fishing tandem flies and the most popular around the country. (See illustration on page 9.) This rig is not complicated. Whenever you want to, add another fly to either your dry or nymph by attaching another length of tippet to the hook bend with a knot such as a clinch or Duncan loop.

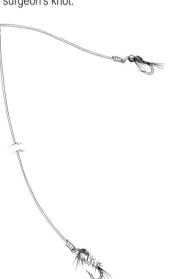

Dropper connection. Connect the first fly to a short section of tippet coming off of the leader, called the dropper, which is formed by intentionally leaving a long tag when you connect the tippets with either a blood or surgeon's knot.

Dropper

Connect the first fly, which can be a dry or a nymph, to a short section of tippet coming off of the leader, called the dropper. The dropper is formed by intentionally leaving a long tag when you connect the tippets with either a blood or surgeon's knot. Several inches to several feet below that, the point, or terminal fly, is tied to the leader's tippet. In this rig, the terminal fly is almost always a nymph or other subsurface pattern. You can use this method with a dry fly, but most anglers use it to fish a series of nymphs, with and without split-shot, fished under an indicator or swung across stream without an indicator.

Dropper Loop

In this old wet-fly rig, you form loops (in a variety of ways) in the leader and connect flies to those loops with loop-to-loop connections or other means. My new looped-leader series of flies allow you to use this rig with an indicator dry fly. This connection allows you to quickly change flies to experiment with different patterns—without having to tie new knots. (See illustration on page 9.)

Two Eye

Connect the first fly and the second fly with two separate leaders through the first fly's eye. For this connection, which is most common with nymphs and streamers, you can get a different action and angle depending on how you connect the two flies, in what I call the T and the angled connections. Because you thread two pieces of tippet through the eye of one hook, this method requires dexterity, good vision, and steady hands.

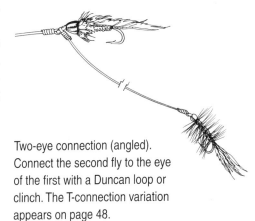

Two-eye connection (angled). Connect the second fly to the eye of the first with a Duncan loop or clinch. The T-connection variation appears on page 48.

Tag

Form this overlooked connection by tying the second fly on a long piece of the tag end remaining after tying on the first fly. This connection is most often used with two subsurface flies.

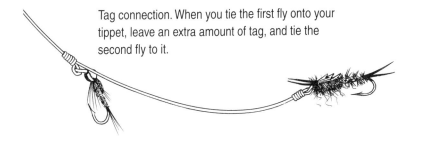

Tag connection. When you tie the first fly onto your tippet, leave an extra amount of tag, and tie the second fly to it.

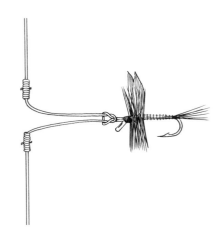

Looped-leader connection. Connect a looped fly to your leader above a knot for a quick way to add or take away flies. For looped-leader tying steps, see page 95.

Looped Leader

This is a new way of connecting flies to either a dropper loop with a loop-to-loop connection or connecting a looped-leader fly to a leader *above* a knot, which prevents the fly from sliding down the leader. You have to tie looped-leader flies in advance, but using this method allows you to quickly add or take away flies depending on conditions.

Movable Dropper

This method is another quick way to attach flies to a leader, as long as your leader has knots in it. You can use it in similar ways to the looped leader, but you don't have to tie looped-leader flies. Instead, tie a piece of 4- to 6-inch tippet to your fly with the knot of your choice. On the other end, tie a Duncan loop and do not pull the loop tight. Slide the loop and fly up over the fly that's already on your leader, position it at a desirable distance from the terminal fly, and cinch the Duncan loop tight.

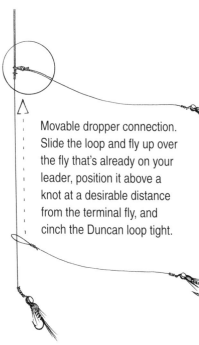

Movable dropper connection. Slide the loop and fly up over the fly that's already on your leader, position it above a knot at a desirable distance from the terminal fly, and cinch the Duncan loop tight.

PATTERN SELECTION

When selecting fly patterns for tandem fishing, I ask the following seven questions:

Will the patterns work in a tandem rig?

I fish multiple flies more than 90 percent of the time. You can fish many flies in a tandem rig, but the best subsurface flies for the type of fishing that I do should sink quickly and be small enough so that they don't sink my favorite indicator fly, the Patriot. Dry flies must be easy to follow on the surface, float well, and be durable enough to catch several fish.

Do I have confidence in the patterns?

I don't know exactly why, but if I believe a pattern will catch trout, it normally does. I don't care how good the pattern is, if you don't believe it will catch trout, you'll probably switch to another pattern shortly. If you are constantly switching patterns, you aren't fishing. I include my confidence patterns in this book, and they may give you some ideas. You'll eventually develop your own list.

Do the patterns work over a wide range of waters and in many conditions?

My patterns need to work over a wide variety of waters and many conditions. For example, the Patriot works as well in New Zealand

From left to right: Hybrid, Trout Fin, White-Winged Bluebird, Patriot. Many of the author's indicator flies imitate mayflies, have prominent calf-hair wings, and plenty of hackle so that they float well.

as it does in the eastern United States. It has caught fish in Labrador and in Bolivia, South America. The Zebra Midge, another on my list, was first developed for Colorado River trout, but it also works well on Pennsylvania, New York, and New Jersey streams.

I also like to have patterns that work under many situations. For high, cloudy water, I have some larger, flashier flies; for low, clear water, smaller ones. One pattern might not be able to do it all—but make sure you have a range of flies to cover the range of water conditions you expect to encounter.

Are the patterns fairly easy to tie?
If you tie your own, this is critical. I've had my fill of woven bodies and other difficult, time-consuming patterns. All the flies I use take just a few minutes to tie—and they catch a lot of fish. Even if you don't tie flies, you can quickly learn how to tie many of the subsurface patterns on my list. You don't have to tie a complicated fly to catch a lot of trout.

Do the flies consistently catch fish?
Some flies lose their magic after a day or two. Maybe it's because I lose faith in them. Though not as glamorous as some other more trendy creations, the Beadhead Pheasant Tail is as effective today as it was when I first started using it, and the venerable Green Weenie catches as many trout today as it did the first time I used it more than fifteen years ago.

Does the fly work year-round?
Flies that have a permanent home in my box catch trout all season long. The Zebra Midge, for instance, works as well midwinter as in summer. I also carry more hatch-specific flies, but the backbone of my box is the patterns I include in this book.

Do the colors cover different light conditions and depths?
To trout, all colors are not equal. Recently scientists have studied the effects of various colors on trout, but many studies are contradictory. Some say trout strike red more; others state that blue is best and that trout see blue flies deeper in the water than most other colors.

I carry both light and dark patterns to make sure that trout can see them under a wide range of lighting conditions (and also that I can see them), and I have designed flies in blue and purple because of studies that say these colors are the last to disappear as the fly sinks deeper in the water column.

DISADVANTAGES

Multiple-fly rigs also mean multiple knots, and rigging tandem flies takes more time than tying on one fly or applying many strike indicators. Some strike indicators attach in seconds, but tying some tandem connections means you have to tie additional knots—additional weak spots in your leader. My looped-leader system is one attempt to speed up the process of assembling a multiple-fly rig. At the end of the day, though, I'd rather take the extra time to rig a dropper than stare at a fluorescent piece of yarn, waiting for a twitch. I use strike indicators for high, fast water or if I need to constantly change the depth at which I fish my nymphs.

Paul Miller gets ready to release a large brown that took a small Beadhead Pheasant Tail trailed behind an indicator fly. The Pheasant Tail is a great pattern to have in your box because, tied in different sizes, it imitates a wide range of trout foods.

I thought the tandem rig was legal on all streams until I fished the Grand River in Ontario, Canada. On this fertile tailwater, anglers are allowed only one fly on the line. I was surprised and unprepared for that, and I wasn't able to fish as well. Make certain you check local regulations before you fish and plan accordingly.

Tandem rigs also tangle easier than one-fly rigs. Even the best casters get tangles, but beginners are particularly prone. Fewer false-casts means fewer tangles. Also, wait until your back cast has almost straightened before beginning your forward cast. You will occasionally foul-hook fish with some tandem rigs. Tandems can tangle in your net when you are landing a fish, and extra hooks mean extra care when you are landing or releasing a fish. But I consider these disadvantages only minor inconveniences compared to the extra fish I catch because of the tandem.

CHAPTER 3

Dry-and-Dropper Rigs

If you've fished with a strike indicator before, you've probably had this experience: you're fishing a nymph under your hot-pink indicator, watching it intently for the slightest twitch, when a trout comes up and tries to eat it. Go figure, you say to yourself. Here you've been fishing for hours without a bite on your ultra-realistic flies, and the trout are committing suicide on your strike indicator. Well, if you use a dry-fly indicator, you stand a good chance of hooking these curious fish, and that's why I call the dry fly a strike indicator with an attitude.

But you're not just taking advantage of reckless trout. Fishing another fly as your strike indicator allows you to cover more bases at once so that you can cover different stages of hatching insects simultaneously, cover different insects hatching at the same time, and meet the tastes of individual trout.

As insects emerge over a period of time, duns float on the water's surface just as nymphs are emerging below. As a hatch builds, different stages of any one particular insect drift throughout the water column. Fish tend to prefer to feed subsurface, but even large trout rise to take surface insects. With a dry-and-dropper rig, you can cover the different stages of a particular insect as it changes from nymph to emerger to dun to spinner.

17

As a hatch builds, different stages of any one particular insect drift throughout the water column. Fish tend to prefer to feed subsurface, but even large trout rise to take surface insects. With multiple flies, you can cover the different stages of a particular insect as it changes from nymph to emerger to dun to spinner.

On many streams, more than one insect species hatches at once. You can improve your chances during these difficult fishing scenarios by fishing different insect species at the same time until you pinpoint what the fish are feeding on. For instance, many anglers fish mayfly duns and midges or mayfly duns and caddis, since caddis and midges are almost ubiquitous food items on many streams.

In addition to matching different stages and different species, tandem flies also improve your chances to catch fish that often have individual tastes. While one fish in the pool may be eating duns on the surface, another fish may be keying on emergers below. Or, one fish may be gulping Pale Morning Dun adults, but another is on the lookout for emerging midge pupae. This is an overlooked, but important, aspect of trout fishing that can potentially be frustrating. Even if you never solve this problem, you can at least mitigate it by using more than one fly.

Though fish are known to feed more subsurface, I've often caught as many fish on the floating pattern as the subsurface one, and those are fish that I wouldn't have caught if I was using a conventional strike indicator. On an average fishing trip, I sometimes catch up to a half-dozen fish on the dry that I never would have caught on the wet. At the end of the day, fishing more flies generally means catching more trout—it's all about odds.

With a dry-and-dropper rig, you can fish one or two flies (or even more) underneath your dry fly. You can use several different strategies for selecting subsurface patterns. If you need weight, at least one of the patterns should be weighted such as a fly with wire wraps tied into it, or a fly with a bead and weighted materials, or a fly that has all of these, such as a Copper John. Maybe you want one fly to be an attractor and the other to be more imitative, or perhaps you want each fly in the rig to imitate different stages of the same insect or different insects altogether.

A dry fly can also be a superior strike detector. Not only does it do a better job of blending in with the stream's surroundings than a fluorescent-red tuft of yarn, most good dry-fly indicator flies transmit subtle takes as well as any strike indicator. Good indicator flies float high on the currents, and though they are not indestructible, they are also not an extra expense or require that you carry extra tackle.

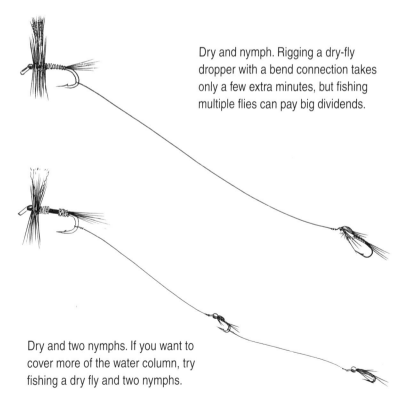

Dry and nymph. Rigging a dry-fly dropper with a bend connection takes only a few extra minutes, but fishing multiple flies can pay big dividends.

Dry and two nymphs. If you want to cover more of the water column, try fishing a dry fly and two nymphs.

While you can adjust the nymph's depth by adding tippet (increasing the distance between the dry and the nymph), if you are fishing a lot of water with varying depths and don't have the desire to retie your rig, an indicator is a much more efficient way to suspend your nymphs. You can just slide an indicator along your tippet to change the depth at which you fish your patterns. With a tandem setup, you have to add or cut tippet unless you are fishing a looped dry fly or movable dropper.

When you are fishing two dry flies or a dry and one or two subsurface patterns, the length of the tippet separating the two flies helps reduce the energy of the mend. If you are fishing an eddy, for instance, and are desperate for a drag-free drift, try fishing two dry flies separated by 16 to 36 inches of tippet. You may twitch the first dry when you mend, but chances are you won't move the second fly. This same principle and technique applies with a dry fly and a nymph.

The white wings on all the flies that I tie as indicator flies readily show up under most conditions. In some high-glare conditions, you might opt for a darker wing. Many patterns have indicator posts with both white and black material for this purpose.

Set the hook if you see the slightest hesitation of the dry fly. The more heavily a stream or river is fished the more apt trout are to strike and leave the scene quickly. Whether using a dry fly or a true strike indicator, you can miss a lot of trout if you are too absorbed with what's going on at the water's surface. Try to follow the wet fly. If you see a trout flash or open its mouth, set the hook. Often, experienced anglers use the dry fly not as an indicator but as a tool to suspend the nymph and look for cues below the water's surface to tell them to set.

Sometimes the water is too high and deep to catch trout on a normal dry-and-dropper rig. In high water, you might consider using two Woolly Buggers or two other large streamer patterns with a dropper loop, bend connection, two-eye, or looped-leader connection. Another alternative is to fish a strike indicator (or a highly buoyant dry fly large enough to float several weighted flies) and two or three weighted nymphs.

HOPPER-DROPPER FISHING

Eric Stroup is one of the finest guides in central Pennsylvania. During the hot summer months Stroup recommends his clients use a hopper and nymph, such as a size 20 Beadhead Pheasant Tail. I recently I watched him fish these two flies on a limestone stream one hot late-July afternoon. Even when there were no trout rising, he caught a half-dozen trout in an hour. Most fish struck within inches of undercut banks, probably because they were holding under the bank to get away from the bright sun. Two took the hopper and four took the nymph.

Hopper-dropper rigs are common in the West, where grasshopper patterns catch lots of large fish in late summer and fall. The East also has some good grasshopper fishing, though the patterns used tend to be smaller than Western ones. Yellow hoppers double as golden stonefly imitations, another popular trout-stream insect. These large patterns, especially deer hair and foam ones, not only imitate the large food items that trout love, but they also float subsurface flies extremely well. Other terrestrials like crickets and beetles also make great indicator flies. To follow the fly easily, pick a pattern that is easy for you to see, such as one with a colorful piece of poly or foam tied on top.

Some anglers, most notably John Barr of Boulder, Colorado, inventor of the Copper John, have taken hopper-dropper fishing to the extreme and often fish two nymphs underneath a

Eric Stroup holds a central Pennsylvania brown that fell for a hopper and Pheasant Tail combination.

A fish taking a hopper pattern is exciting, but not all fish will come to the surface for a hopper fly, as tasty as it might look. The hopper pattern is buoyant and is easy to see on the surface, making it an excellent indicator fly to detect strikes on the nymph below.

highly buoyant foam hopper. Barr calls this system the Hopper Copper Dropper. Barr often uses a heavily weighted Copper John as his second fly to help sink the rig, then attaches a hatch-matching emerger, nymph, or pupa to the bend of the Copper John. The theory is that fish are attracted to the flash and glitz of the Copper John, but they take the more realistic pattern dangling in front of them. Though large foam hoppers with rubber legs are more suitable for Western waters, smaller patterns are perfectly appropriate

Hoppers tied with foam float well and are durable. Choose flies with bright foam or yarn on top so that you can see them easily in riffles and poor light.

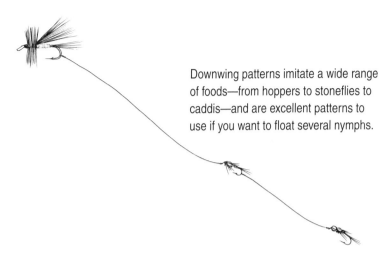

Downwing patterns imitate a wide range of foods—from hoppers to stoneflies to caddis—and are excellent patterns to use if you want to float several nymphs.

for Eastern waters if you want to experiment with more than one fly beneath the hopper.

Hoppers and other large or heavily hackled fly patterns are excellent for fishing in faster, choppy water with broken currents. In this type of water, fish don't have as long to scrutinize your fly, so you can get away with more heavily dressed patterns, which you'll need for those currents. Larger flies are also easier for you to see in riffles, whereas flush-floating patterns can be difficult to detect. Flush-floating patterns such as Parachute Adams will work in riffles but are most often a better choice for slower currents.

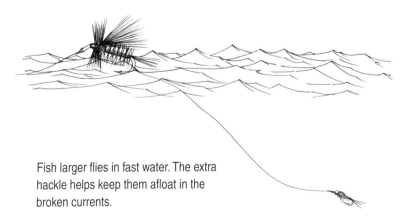

Fish larger flies in fast water. The extra hackle helps keep them afloat in the broken currents.

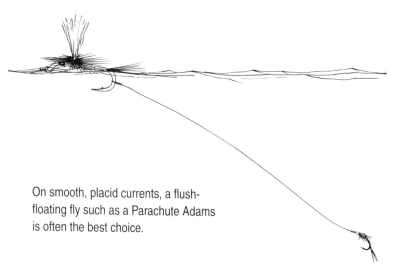

On smooth, placid currents, a flush-floating fly such as a Parachute Adams is often the best choice.

Dry flies become waterlogged from bobbing in the currents and slimed from hooked fish, and it's critical that you treat your flies so that they float well. Different treatments are effective for different flies. You can treat most flies with a conventional floatant, and you should do so—even your foam flies. I use a facial cleanser called Albolene to float the fly (one jar will last a long time), but most fly dressings will do. After catching some fish on the pattern, use

Royal Wulffs (left) and Humpies (right) are great indicator flies, especially for brook trout or cutthroat in faster water, and imitate a wide range of mayflies.

Above: Terrestrials and Tricos are midsummer's main game on many trout streams around the country. To make your terrestrials easy to see, tie or buy ones with bright yarn or fluorescent paint on top.

Right: The Stimulator and variations cover a wide range of hoppers and downwings.

Shimizake or another dessicant to bring the materials back to life. You can pretreat your flies with floatant at home to save time in the field and to make sure that it has time to permeate the materials. If you are fishing CDC patterns, do not add floatant to the CDC unless it is natural and made from the preen oil of CDC feathers. Many anglers will apply Frogs Fanny to these types of patterns. To revive them after catching a few fish, rinse them in water and press them between an amadou or buckskin patch.

Yes, a dry-fly indicator is bound to occasionally hang up on the leader and create a tangle in your line that is almost always faster to cut out, and it's an extra fly to lose if your rig gets caught in the bushes. It also requires that you adjust your casting stroke, and it's one more hook to catch your finger when you're releasing a fish. But, in my experience, the pros far outweigh these cons.

CHAPTER 4

Other Combinations

Fishing a dry and one or two nymphs is one possible combination. You can also fish two wet flies or two dry flies. You can even fish three (or more) wet flies or one dry and two wets, if the wets are small or if the dry fly is large and floats well. You are limited only by your fly selection and imagination.

TWO DRY FLIES

As I've grown older, I have more difficulty following a size 24 dry fly on the surface, especially if the flies float flush on the surface such as spent spinners. Fishing two dry flies at once can help solve this problem. Tie an easy to-see dry fly as your indicator fly and a size 24 Trico or other small pattern off the bend on 16 to 24 inches of tippet. Follow the indicator fly to help predict the smaller fly's location.

Two dry flies aren't just for older anglers. Many experienced midge fishermen use larger flies to help them track their miniscule patterns. Small dark terrestrials (or other patterns) are also hard to detect. If the trout are finicky, use a smaller dry. A size 18 indicator fly is still easier to see than a drab little size 24. Use the first dry to help gauge the location of the second fly, and set the hook if there is a disturbance in the water near where you think your fly is or if the indicator fly hesitates or twitches.

Fish a dry fly 16 to 24 inches in front of your spinner to help you track it.

Fishing two dry flies also helps you cover more bases if you don't know what surface flies fish are feeding on. A few years back I was on the river during a fantastic Sulphur hatch in which flies emerged for more than a half hour and trout fed with frenzy. In addition to the duns, Sulphur spinners rode the surface, laying eggs before they died. Some trout fed barely underneath the surface on emerging duns while others ate floating, dying spinners. Because I couldn't figure out exactly which phase fish were feeding on, I tied a spinner pattern to the bend of my dun. That evening I caught several trout on each fly, and the experience taught me a valuable lesson: If you're not certain of the insect phase trout are taking, try several at the same time.

SUNKEN DRY FLIES

After bobbing along on the water's currents, many insects sink. The spent Trico spinners that have floated in fast water downriver for a mile eventually end up under the surface, where fish continue to feed on them. Sometimes the largest trout feed on sunken insects. To catch difficult fish, I often fish a weighted spinner below a dry fly during and after a spinner fall, especially below riffles where the broken currents may have submerged spinners. Several species of mayflies also dive underneath the water to lay their eggs.

If I live to be a hundred, I'll never forget the lesson an old angler taught me more than thirty years ago on Falling Springs Branch, near Chambersburg, Pennsylvania. I've written and talked about this incident many times, but it deserves to be restated. This old man kept catching one trout after another (at least seven fish) during a Trico spinner fall. I fished a hundred feet away and across

Don't overlook the importance of sunken spinners. Fish a weighted spinner behind a dry fly during and after a spinner fall.

stream from him, and in an hour I managed to land one small, wild fish. I cast my size 24 Trico over every riser in the area. When he caught his eighth trout, I had enough. I called out to him over the riffled water and asked him what fly he was using. He didn't answer me, and I thought the old man was partially deaf, the stream's din muffled my voice, or he was ignoring me. In about ten minutes the spinner fall ended, and the old man wound up his line and headed for his car.

As he turned and walked away, he muttered four words that still haunt me today: "I'm sinking the fly." He never once looked at me.

I pondered the man's words on my two-hour trip home that afternoon. Then it came to me: That old codger was fishing his Trico spinner pattern under the surface as a wet fly. It made a lot of sense. Some of the spinners sank. Why not tie some patterns to copy them? I tied a half-dozen spent-wing wet flies, adding five wraps of lead wire to the hook shanks, and looked forward to using them soon.

But soon didn't happen for more than a decade. In early August 2002, 2,000 miles away from Falling Springs Branch, Jerry Armstrong and I were committed to teach a one-week fly-fishing program on the Ruby River at Upper River Outfitters near Alder, Montana. I arrived at the lodge one day before the workshop to get the lay of the land and to fish the river. I arrived on the Ruby around 8:30 A.M. and diminutive, clear-wing Trico spinners already filled the cool morning air. Wind gusts blew them into my mouth. When the females started landing on the surface, the trout began to rise. I began casting and casting, but nothing I used worked.

Tricos are so small that you can design a sinking fly by tying it on a heavy-wire hook and keeping the profile streamlined.

Within minutes after I started fishing, several registrants for next day's class wandered down to watch their instructor. The pressure was on. Tomorrow, I planned a talk based on my book *How To Catch More Trout*. I fished for 5 minutes, 10 minutes, 15 minutes—and couldn't catch a trout. My students could probably sense my discouragement. Would they listen to anything I said in the upcoming program if I couldn't catch any of these trout? I glanced over at the group across the river, and I saw them whispering to each other. What would I do? How could I teach the class tomorrow to people who clearly saw I couldn't catch one trout, let alone *more* trout?

Then, I had an idea. Since there were only a few trout rising during this dense spinner fall, I thought about trying one of the sunken spinners I had tied up years ago. I dug through my box of Tricos and found the weighted patterns—still intact—that I had tied fifteen years ago. I quickly tied one on 24 inches of tippet to the bend of a size 16 Patriot and began casting. On the second cast, the Patriot sank, and I set the hook on a 12-inch rainbow. Two more casts, and I caught another trout on the spinner. By the sixth trout, the group across the river began applauding. I was safe for tomorrow.

Another way to catch fish during the summer doldrums is to fish sunken terrestrials. Terrestrials fall into the water all the time, and those that don't swim to shore often end up under the water. I have fished weighted ant and beetle patterns for years. I add a copper bead as the front hump of a cinnamon ant pattern to sink it quickly. Many anglers overlook sunken grasshopper and cricket imitations, but trout don't.

WET FLIES

You can fish two or more wet flies under a large dry fly, under an indicator, or without an indicator—especially if you are swinging flies, like the older method of fishing a cast of wet flies downstream. The most popular connections for nymphs are bend connections, two eye, or droppers, but you can also connect looped-leader nymphs to dropper loops or to knotted leaders (placed just above a knot).

There are several effective configurations for fishing nymphs, depending on the circumstances. You can first tie on a heavily weighted pattern to sink the rig, followed by a pattern that floats freely in the currents. I'll often fish a weighted Beadhead Pheasant Tail with a Zebra Midge tied to the bend. The weighted fly gets the rig deep, and the unweighted midge pattern drifts freely above the heavy fly. Many anglers have one or two specialty flies that they like to use for this purpose. The best patterns are generic enough so that you can use them throughout the season and sink quickly—the Copper John is an excellent example of a generic pattern that can also be used as a weighted first fly. The second option is to first tie on the smaller pattern followed by the larger, weighted one.

A heavily weighted pattern such as the Copper John can take the place of split-shot if you are fishing subsurface flies. Charlie Craven photo

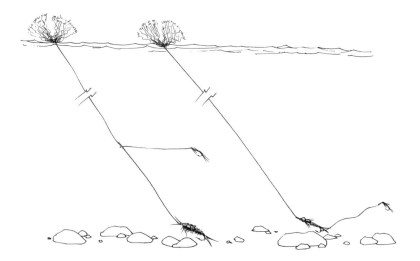

When fishing heavily weighted flies in fast currents, strike indicators are often a better choice than indicator flies. You can rig your flies in many different ways. The dropper (left) and bend connections (right) may be the most popular.

The setup you choose may depend on what you have already tied on. For instance, if you are fishing a heavy nymph but want to cover another area in the water column with an emerger, you may just attach the emerger above the tippet knot with a movable dropper, or retie the fly, leaving a tag large enough to attach the emerger. If you don't feel like rerigging, you can attach the emerger to the bend of the heavy nymph. There are always several available options with these combinations, and you should experiment and let the trout tell you which one they like best.

In the Czech-nymphing style of fishing, anglers fish heavily weighted, streamlined nymphs (so that they sink quickly), most often three at a time. They connect two nymphs on droppers and one on point and most often tie the heaviest fly pattern on the middle dropper, so that the weighted fly helps sink both the first dropper and the point fly.

Fishing several subsurface patterns is often a better choice in high water than fishing a dry-and-dropper rig. Though the dry-and-dropper rig is versatile, it is best for water depths from one to four feet and slower to medium currents. In high, fast water, fish one or more weighted nymphs under a supersized indicator fly or indicator. The downside of using a fly large enough to float these weighted flies—like some of the foam hopper and stoneflies popular in the West—is that they can be less aerodynamic to cast than some strike indicators—though large polypropylene yarn indicators are no joy to cast. Fast-action rods and line weights and leader tapers designed for turning over heavier, wind-resistant flies make casting large foam hoppers, stoneflies, and Chernobyl Ant-style patterns relatively painless.

STREAMERS

Fishing two streamers is a deadly way to entice the largest fish to strike. The two most popular connections for fishing tandem streamers are the bend and two-eye connections. When fishing streamers, choose flies with different colors and sizes. Fish one fly that is smaller than the other, and fish flies that are both light and dark to cover as many bases as possible. Woolly Buggers are always good choices to imitate large hellgrammites, stonefly nymphs, as well as crayfish and sculpins, and you can't go wrong with rabbit-

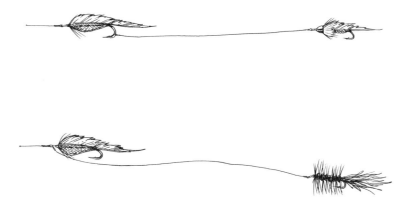

Two popular ways of connecting tandem streamers are the bend (top) and two-eye connections (bottom). Some anglers think that streamers have more action with the two-eye connection, though I find it easier to tie tippet on to the bend of a hook than through a hook eye already crowded with tippet.

strip flies such as Zonkers or Double Bunnies. You don't cast two streamers as much as you lob them. It isn't pretty, but the combination is deadly. Two of my favorite Woolly Bugger variations are the Beadhead Woolly Bugger and Rooke's Minnow.

The easiest setup for fishing multiple streamers from a drift boat is a short sinking-tip line with a floating running line and a short, straight piece of tippet heavy enough to help turn over the flies, prevent break offs when fish slam your fly, and stout enough to pull your flies from snags or the occasional bush as you pound the banks. Fish typically aren't leader shy with streamers because they often see the fly first and the fly is generally fished on an active retrieve.

In addition to an active retrieve, a combination of dead-drifting and short strips also works well. Many anglers fish tandem streamers with a floating line and tapered leader. Good casting technique is essential with this setup, as is the leader's taper design. Use weight-forward lines with heavy front tapers (nymph and bass tapers) and leaders with large butt diameters that extend through at least half of

This heavy rainbow took a dark-colored conehead rabbit-strip fly trailed behind a white Zonker. When fishing tandem streamers, make sure that you fish two flies with different sizes, colors, or actions to cover more bases.

the entire leader's length. When fishing double streamers, it's imperative to modify your casting stroke, not only to prevent tangles, but to prevent hitting yourself with the heavy flies (see page 69).

Though many anglers don't use them, streamer and nymph combinations also work well, perhaps because the larger streamer draws the fish's attention to the nymph. On central Oregon's Deschutes River I had a great five-mile float casting a Woolly Bugger and *Pteronarcys* stonefly imitation in tandem. Thousands of huge stonefly nymphs crawled out of the water, and we caught lots of fish dead-drifting and twitching this rig as we floated downriver.

CHAPTER 5

Connections

The most common way of connecting two flies is in-line with the bend connection, but other ways are effective depending on the situation. I write about seven ways, and I'm certain there are more. The most popular are the bend connection, dropper loop, dropper, tag, and two eye. Two that I've discovered relatively recently are the looped leader and movable dropper. Many of these connections have been around for ages, but some, like the movable dropper and looped-leader connections, are relatively new—or at least new modifications of older rigs.

Though I most frequently use the bend and looped-leader connections, experimenting with some of these other connections has expanded my angling repertoire and has helped me catch more fish under different circumstances. Depending on your needs—and your style of fishing—you may find that another one of these connections will serve you better. It's worth learning them all.

BEND

The bend connection is a great way to fish two flies, and most guides I know prefer it over any other connection. This connection simply calls for attaching each additional fly to the bend of the one in front of it. It works well with two dry flies, a dry fly and one or

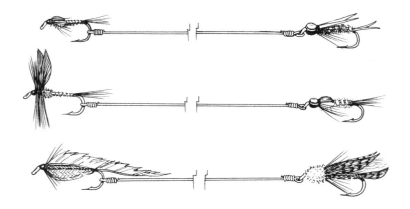

You can use the bend connection with two nymphs, a dry fly and a nymph, or two streamers.

more nymphs, all nymphs, or streamers—probably why most people favor this connection.

I'll use the dry fly as the lead fly in my example, but the same principles apply for streamers or nymphs. First connect your tippet to the eye of the dry fly hook with the knot of your choice. I like to use a Duncan loop pulled tight. Once the first fly is secure, take a 16- to 36-inch length of tippet (or another length determined by the depth you want to fish) and attach it to the bend of the dry fly hook with either a Duncan loop (uni knot) cinched tight or improved clinch. Then attach the tippet's free end to the eye of the wet fly.

If the tippet to the dry fly is 5X, then I use 5X or 6X tippet to connect the wet fly to the dry. I like to use fluorocarbon tippet to connect both the dry fly and the subsurface ones. Fluorocarbon sinks more than monofilament, and it helps the wet flies sink faster, but I don't think it has much effect on the dry fly—at least the large, buoyant dry flies that I use as indicator flies.

Besides being easy to tie, the bend connection is an excellent choice when your indicator fly is front heavy. The weight of the dropper nymph helps anchor the dry and keep it floating upright. One downside of this popular connection is that when trout try to strike the first fly they often feel the leader connecting the two pat-

Pretie tandem setups with bend connections and wrap them around pipe insulating foam. You can rig several combinations ahead of time.

terns. At the last minute, some of the trout veer away and can get foul-hooked by the second fly.

Knots to Know

One reason why the clinch (or improved clinch) is a popular knot to tie tippet to the hook bend is that it is easier for most people to tie than the Duncan loop, though the Duncan loop is stronger. To tie a quick and easy clinch, tie it on your finger first. Twist the leader five times with your finger to form the loop and the turns and then pass the tag end through the large loop, slip the loop over point and onto the bend of the first fly, and pull tight. If you tie the knot on the fly, turn the hook upside down so that the loop at the bottom of the knot doesn't slide off the hook as you try to thread the tag.

The improved and regular clinch knots, though popular, are weak knots. However, the clinch is easy to remember and easy to tie correctly, so overall, it's a pretty good knot. Remember, a knot is only as good as it is tied, and a strong knot tied poorly can be worse than a weak knot tied well. Modern tippet materials are so strong that you can't put enough pressure on most trout to break a properly tied clinch. The knot fails for other reasons.

For connecting flies to tippet and for tying tippet to hook bends, I prefer the uni knot (also called the Duncan loop) for its strength and versatility. You can use this knot to attach your backing to your arbor, fly to tippet, and leader butt to fly line (also called the speed nail knot). It's handy to know for those reasons alone, but you can also use it as a loop or cinch it completely tight. When using it as a bend connection on the tandem, you can pretie the loops and cinch them tight when you need them or open up the loops to remove the tippet from the hook bend if you are changing rigs or switching to a single fly. (See the instructions for tying the Duncan loop on page 53.)

DROPPER
This connection requires some advance planning. When you tie your last or second-to-last leader segment (the one you select depends on the depth of the wet fly), leave a three- to six-inch piece and connect the dry fly to that tag end. For example, you connect a 4X to a 5X tip-

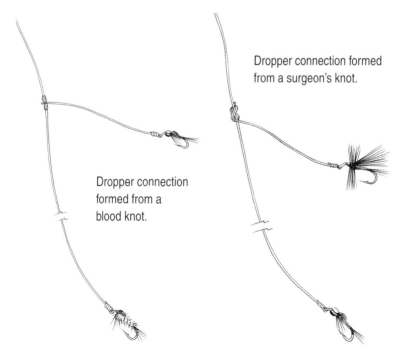

Dropper connection formed from a surgeon's knot.

Dropper connection formed from a blood knot.

pet for the last two sections of your leader. Make the 4X three to six inches longer than needed. Use a triple surgeon's knot to connect the two leaders and don't cut the excess 4X, which now becomes home for the dry fly or another wet. Tie the point fly (usually a wet fly) to the end of the 5X tippet. If you want the wet fly to go deeper, add another section to your 5X tippet. If you feel more comfortable with using a blood knot, you can use that as well.

I first used this connection on the McKenzie River in Oregon and found that with longer casts, this rig is prone to tangling. You can reduce this by using stiffer monofilament like Maxima or fluorocarbon and keeping the dropper tippet less than six inches. Longer than that increases the chances of the fly twisting around the leader. Because this is not a straight connection like the bend connection, a fish's strike has to transmit from the point fly to the leader to the tippet of the lead fly. I think this makes it harder to detect strikes quickly.

To connect multiple nymphs, tie in multiple sections of tippet. You can also crimp split-shot onto the tippet instead of a terminal fly and use nymphs on the droppers. That way, when you hang up, you only lose the split-shot, and the split-shot rolls over rocks better than a nymph. This setup allows to you fish deep, snags less, and you can change any one of the flies without rerigging.

Knots to Know

Use blood or surgeon's knots to connect your tippet and form the droppers. When I use surgeon's knots, I use the double surgeon's on all leader connections, except for the last one connecting the two lightest or thinnest leader sections where I tie a triple.

The surgeon's is easier for me to tie than a blood, and that's why I prefer it. I lost part of my finger in an accident with a folding chair while I sat at my computer working on *Pennsylvania Trout Streams and Their Hatches*. Since then, I have been unable to tie a blood knot. Both the blood and surgeon's knots have about the same strength, but the surgeon's knot has one distinct disadvantage. If you're replacing a middle piece of your leader, and the fly is still attached to the tippet, you have to bring the leader and fly through the opening two or three times. You don't have to do that with a blood knot.

The surgeon's knot is simple to tie. Overlap the two pieces of leader you want to connect by three or four inches. Make a loop in the two and bring both leaders (not the one connected to the fly line) through the loop two or three times.

A triple surgeon's is much stronger than a double. Gary Borger came up with an easy way to tie the double that I've dubbed "one, two, and put it through." And I've modified that for a triple: "One, two, three, and let it be." Overlap the two leaders by four inches, wrap the two around hemostat jaws three times, and pull the ends through the opening with the forceps. Use the triple surgeon's for finer tippets and a double for leader sections over 6- to 8-pound-test.

DROPPER LOOP

Attaching multiple flies with dropper loops is an old technique, and one that I've seen used for more than sixty years. With looped-leader flies or flies with a short tippet and loop, it is simple to connect your fly with a loop-to-loop connection. If you want to experiment with other patterns, perhaps no other method is faster. This rig is most popular with anglers who fish all wet flies. However, you can use a dry fly as your lead fly. If you want to dead-drift the nymphs instead of swinging them like the old-timers, you can use a strike indicator with this rig. In this method, the loops are permanent, and a correctly tied dropper loop comes off the leader at a right angle.

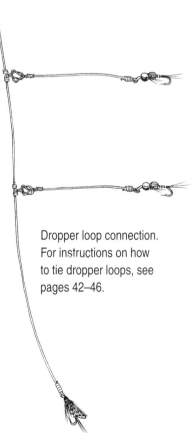

Dropper loop connection. For instructions on how to tie dropper loops, see pages 42–46.

There are many effective ways to tie the dropper loop, and I will touch on four that I've taken the liberty of naming: overhand knot, blood knot, matchstick, and speed dropper.

Knots to Know
Overhand Knot Dropper
When I teach people to tie a dropper loop, I usually show them the overhand knot method, because it is easy to understand and involves movements that people are used to. To form this knot, make a loop in the line and pass the end of the leader through the loop and around one side of it five times. Open the middle of the

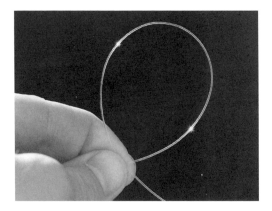

Form a loop in the leader where you want the finished dropper loop.

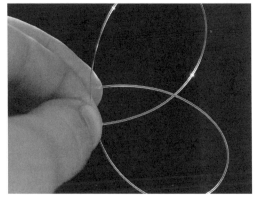

Pass the end of the leader or tippet through the loop and begin wrapping it around one side of the leader.

Make five wraps around the leader. In the illustration, the end is short, but if you want a loop 16 inches from the end of the tippet, you have to thread all 16 inches of leader and tippet through the loop and wrap it around the leader.

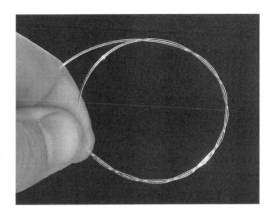

Find and separate the center of the wraps. Reach through them and grasp the top of the loop with your fingers or forceps.

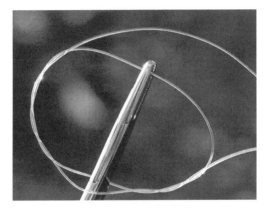

Pull the top of the loop through the center of the wraps.

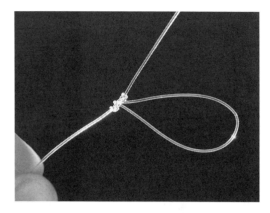

Moisten and tighten the knot.

twists with your fingers or hemostats, and thread the line through this loop. Wet the wraps and pull tight. This technique requires you to pass the end of the tippet through the loop, which can be cumbersome if there is a fly attached.

Blood Knot Dropper

When you are connecting two tippets, you can form a dropper loop in the line by tying a blood knot. Double over one of the pieces of tippet the same way that you would tie the improved blood knot commonly used for attaching tippets of dissimilar sizes. Do not trim the loop.

Matchstick Dropper

The advantage of this method is that you can tie a fast dropper loop anywhere in your leader without untying your fly. (See illustration on page 45.) Form a loop in the leader, place a match or short stick at the junction, and twist it five times. Pass the top end of the loop through the hole the match holds open. Moisten and pull tight.

Speed Dropper

This method requires a little practice and some dexterity and is basically the matchstick dropper knot without the matchstick. When you are cinching everything tight, it helps if you use your mouth as well as both hands. (See illustration on page 46.)

Matchstick dropper.

Form a loop in the line and place a matchstick as shown.

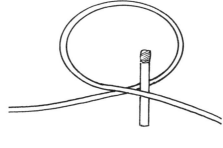

Begin twisting the matchstick, forming the knot.

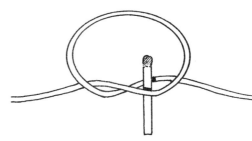

After five twists, remove the match and hold the hole open.

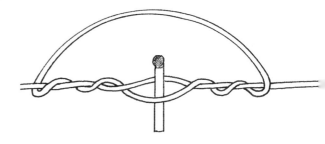

Pass the top of the loop through the hole and pull tight. The finished knot should look like the one on page 44.

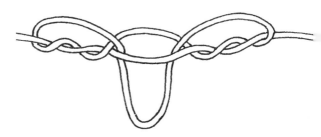

Speed dropper.

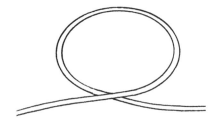

Form a loop. In these steps, the side closest to the tippet passes under the end closest to the leader, but you can form the loop the other way.

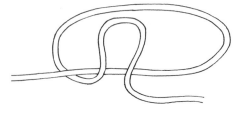

Form a smaller loop with the line leading to the tippet and wrap that loop over and through the larger loop forming the twists in the line. In this method you are replicating the steps for the matchstick dropper, without the matchstick.

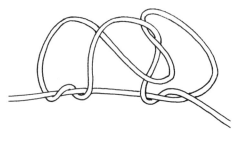

Pass the top of the large loop through the hole, which is also the smaller loop.

Pull tight. It helps to use your mouth and both hands.

The finished knot.

Connecting the Flies

Once you have formed the dropper loops, either at home or onstream, you can connect the flies to the loops several ways. You can either connect the fly directly to the loop by 1) passing the loop through the eye of the fly or 2) using a looped fly. You can also use flies that have a short length of tippet already attached to them with loops on the ends and connect them loop to loop. Tie the loops with either a perfection loop, surgeon's loop, or nonslip loop. Or, you can bypass the loop-to-loop connection and attach the fly and tippet to the loop with a clinch knot.

Connecting Fly Directly to the Loop

The easiest way to do this is to use a looped-leader fly. Pass the dropper loop through the loop on the fly and around the fly, and pull them tight. The hard way is to thread the loop through the hook eye. This method is not desirable, but it can be done if you have a fly with an eye that's big enough or you use some type of threader to pull the loop through the eye. In both of these instances, the tippet for the dropper loop must be thin diameter. Once you pass the loop through the fly eye, bring the loop around the fly and pull tight.

Connecting Tippet to Loop with Loop to Loop

This method is how many used to connect tandem flies. Flies came snelled with a short length of tippet that had a loop on one end. By connecting the loops, you could easily change your flies. Instead of snelling your flies, you can attach them with a knot of your choice and then tie a fixed loop knot such as a perfection, surgeon's, or nonslip loop on the other end of the tippet.

Attach Directly with Clinch Knot

This is a fast connection, but it bypasses the purpose of a loop. Just pretend the dropper loop is a very large hook eye and tie a short piece of tippet to it with a clinch or improved clinch knot. Tie your fly on the other end.

TWO EYE

Some anglers connect the tippet of the lead fly and the tippet from the point fly through the eye of the lead fly. The larger the fly (and the larger the hook eye) the larger diameter tippet you can use. For small flies, it's essential to use 5X to 7X tippet to fit both knots in the hook eye, or use big-eye hooks available from some manufacturers. This rig is most often used with wet flies.

T-Connection

The angle at which you attach the tippet to the hook eye is important in the two-eye connection. In the T-connection version of the two-eye connection for nymphs, the first tippet is attached to the side of the eye of the first nymph and the second tippet (that leads to the second nymph) to the other side of the eye so that the first nymph is perpendicular to the tippet. Connect the second nymph as you would any other pattern.

Angled Connection

You can also attach the flies at an angle, which is effective for streamers. Many anglers think that when you strip the fly, the second streamer has more action than if the connection was in line and off the hook bend. In this configuration, the tippet comes off the eye at a 45-degree angle. The first streamer is tied straight.

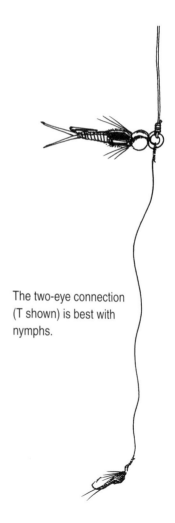

The two-eye connection (T shown) is best with nymphs.

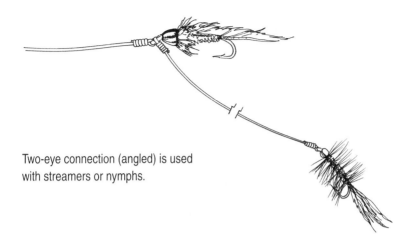

Two-eye connection (angled) is used
with streamers or nymphs.

TAG

When you connect your tippet to a fly, you typically cut off the
excess tippet (or tag) after you tie the knot. Some anglers intentionally leave a long tag when they tie the tippet to the fly and tie
another fly onto it.

This simple but overlooked connection only requires two knots—
one less than most of the others—so you have potentially fewer knots
that can fail on you, and rigging it is quick and easy. Like many of the
connections that go through the fly eye, the tag end sometimes top-

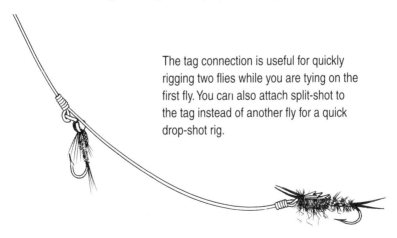

The tag connection is useful for quickly
rigging two flies while you are tying on the
first fly. You can also attach split-shot to
the tag instead of another fly for a quick
drop-shot rig.

ples the lead fly if it's a dry fly. I don't prefer this connection when I use dry flies, but if you want to use it you can overcome the toppling effect by making the tails of your dry flies heavier and longer, or use flush-floating foam patterns, Stimulators, or Parachutes for your indicator flies.

This connection is also a great way to fish a single nymph and split-shot on the tag end. The nymph rides above the stream bottom free from snags as the split-shot bounces along. Tie a figure-8 knot in the tag to keep the shot from sliding off.

LOOPED LEADER

I developed a pattern called the looped-leader fly (see tying instructions on page 95). It is a bit like the old snelled wet fly, but shorter, with a finer leader, and I designed it primarily for dry flies. Even if you are not fishing tandem flies, a few looped-leader flies come in handy at or near dark when a supersize fly eye makes tying on flies a snap in the failing light. To connect the looped-leader fly to the leader, make a loop with your leader just above a knot. Thread the leader loop through the loop on the fly and bring the leader over the body of the looped fly to secure.

You can move the looped fly up your leader to temporarily change the depth of the wet fly for a cast or two. However, the dry fly slips down to the knot after a few casts. To form a knot in your leader so that you

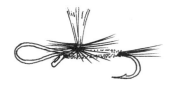

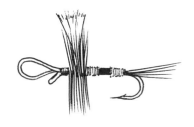

You can add loops to most fly patterns. From top to bottom: Looped-Leader Parachute Adams, Looped-Leader Hare's Ear, Looped-Leader Patriot.

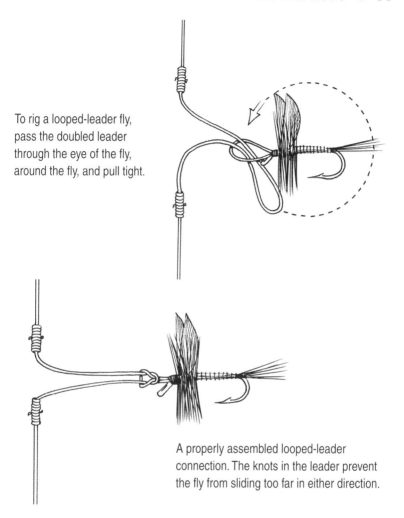

To rig a looped-leader fly, pass the doubled leader through the eye of the fly, around the fly, and pull tight.

A properly assembled looped-leader connection. The knots in the leader prevent the fly from sliding too far in either direction.

can change depth permanently, cut off your tippet and reattach with a blood or surgeon's knot. If you are using a tapered, knotted leader, chances are you'll have knots spaced along your leader.

This method of attaching flies is quick—perhaps faster than any other method—though preparing the flies takes some time, and you must tie your own or have someone tie them for you. The loop is strong if you tie it into the fly properly, and I have never broken a loop on a fish.

For difficult or wary trout, the relatively large loop and loop-to-loop connection might not be the best choice, but this is a good method if you are using the dry fly primarily as a strike indicator and way to suspend your nymphs. Looped flies don't seem to tangle the leader as quickly as some other rigs, and I think I hook more trout with this method than some others because setting the hook is more direct. To compensate for the extra weight at the end of some flies—like my Patriot—I tie long tails. The loop on the fly can be one-quarter inch to several inches long. Ideally the diameter of the tippet you use for the loop on the fly should match the tippet diameter on your leader. You can also use this system with nymphs.

MOVABLE DROPPER

The movable dropper combines the looped-leader concept and the dropper—but because you don't have to tie a loop into the fly, it is easy to rig onstream. Eric Stroup has taught his clients this method for years. Take a 4- to 6-inch piece of 4X to 6X fluorocarbon, tie one end of that piece through the eye of the lead fly, and secure it with a Duncan loop (uni knot). (See diagram on page 53.) Take the other end of the leader, tie a Duncan loop on it, and don't pull it tight. Prepare some ahead of time, and leave the loop large enough so that you can slip it over the point fly. Take the open Duncan loop and slide it over the point fly up the leader, and cinch it tight just above a knot on the leader so it doesn't slide down.

If you are using a knotless leader, to make the point fly go deeper, form a new knot and place the movable dropper just above

The first step for rigging a movable dropper is to form the dropper. Tie a Duncan loop on the end of a short piece of tippet connected to the fly you want to position on your leader.

it, add a piece of leader to the section connecting the point fly, or move the dropper up the leader and form a temporary knot held in place by a small piece of toothpick. To do this, form a slip knot and place a short piece of toothpick (which swells when wet) in it. If your point fly is a nymph, you can also crimp a small split-shot to the tippet to keep the movable dropper in place.

Alleviate tangles with the dropper by using 3X or 4X fluorocarbon tippets instead of 5X or 6X monofilament, and use no more than 4 inches of tippet. The short length also helps you set the hook more quickly when using a dry-fly indicator.

Knots to Know

The Duncan loop is stronger than the improved clinch, and with practice, you'll find it as easy to tie. Place the tippet through the hook eye and double it over itself. Make a loop with the tag end of the tippet, wrap the tag end of the tippet over the doubled strands and through the loop five times, and pull tight. Don't pull the knot tight if you want the fly to move. To help the knot close, wet it before pulling tight.

I prefer using the looped leader, movable dropper, bend, and tag systems. The movable dropper, looped leader, dropper, two eye,

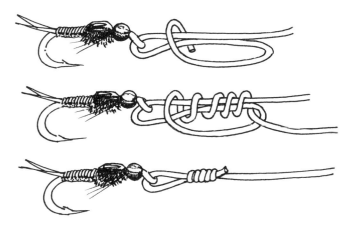

Duncan loop steps. One of the benefits of this knot is that you can pull it tight like a clinch or leave an open loop for more action.

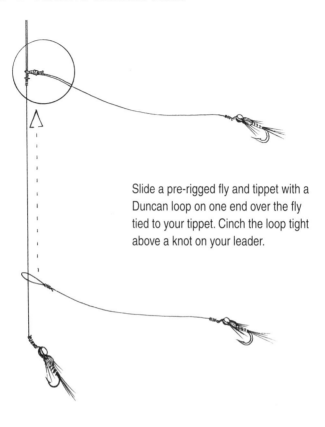

Slide a pre-rigged fly and tippet with a Duncan loop on one end over the fly tied to your tippet. Cinch the loop tight above a knot on your leader.

and tag tend to cause the dry fly to ride on its head. To eliminate this, or at least minimize it, make the tails of these flies longer and heavier. If presentation of the dry is important, then the bend connection is probably your best choice.

CHAPTER 6

Tackle and Techniques

In this chapter, I'm going to discuss special issues with tackle that I feel are directly related to fishing tandem flies as well as different techniques that I find helpful, including casting and mending techniques, when fishing multiple-fly rigs.

TACKLE

I'm not going to cover all aspects of fishing tackle—many good books already do that—but I'll discuss a few critical components for tandem rigs: your rod, leaders and tippets, and knots. If you are just beginning fly fishing, I recommend you read some general books on tackle. With tandem flies, you'll be tying a lot of knots, so it's imperative that you learn how to tie a few basic ones correctly and efficiently. Study knot guides and practice, practice, practice— preferably at home and not onstream. At home you can concentrate on learning the knot, whereas on the water you'll be too preoccupied with fishing.

Rods

I normally use a fairly stiff 9-foot, 5-weight graphite fly rod. Too often, when fishing soft-action rods, I can't get enough hook-setting power. You need to take up all the slack in the system—line, leader, fly, and the tippet connecting the flies—quickly enough to set the

To consistently catch fish, technique and tackle must work together. On spring creeks and tailwaters such as the South Platte in Colorado (above), big fish eat small flies, so your rig must not only be capable of tricking these difficult fish but also landing them.

hook on a fish. Soft-action rods bend too much before taking in that slack, whereas a fast-action rod is more responsive. Also, I hate casting two flies with wet noodles—rods that flex from butt to tip. But that's just a personal preference. Some prefer slow-action rods for fishing wet flies.

Longer rods help me cast farther and mend line more effectively and efficiently to get longer drifts. When I fish small streams, I often opt for a shorter rod matched for a lighter line weight and a 7-foot leader. On smaller streams with tighter quarters, it's easier to cast and maneuver a shorter line and leader.

I leave my rod rigged and ready in the back of my car through the fishing season so I spend more time fishing and less time rigging, at least for local trips. I realize that this might not be practical for many and some are simply too protective of their tackle, but it saves me time. Some guides rig several rods with tandem flies—for instance, one rod with a dry and a dropper and one with two streamers—and keep them ready in the boat so their clients spend more time fishing.

Leaders

A tapered leader's function is to get the fly on the water, where you want it, with as little commotion as possible. A tapered leader (one with a heavier butt section slowly progressing to a smaller diameter tippet) will turn the fly over, yet—if it is built properly—helps it land delicately on the water with enough S-curves to prevent drag.

All tapered leaders have three main sections: butt (section closest to the fly line), midsection, and tippet. For fishing tandem flies, I like to use leaders built with 60 percent butt, 20 percent midsection, and 20 percent tippet. I usually start with a stiff butt section of .021-, .019-, or .017-inch-diameter Maxima or Mason to help turn over the flies. If you are using store-bought leaders, buy ones with butts that closely match your fly line's diameter to help turn over the leader. I use tippets about 24 inches long, sometimes a bit longer, in clear, low water. When I connect flies, I often reduce the tippet size from one fly to the next. For instance, if I connect a dry fly with 4X tippet, I connect the nymph with 5X. I typically fish leaders around 9½ feet long, though you can go shorter in tight brush or a wind, or longer if the fish are spooky. If you buy leaders then purchase 7½-foot ones with a 2X, 3X, or 4X tippet. Cut a bit of the original tippet and tie on 24 inches of 3X, 4X, or 5X fluorocarbon tippet.

Knotless leaders are smooth and tapered. Knotted leaders include sections that are different diameters connected with blood or surgeon's knots. I think knotted leaders turn over better than knotless ones, though I like to use knotless leaders when fishing in water with lots of algae and weeds, which can collect around knots.

Knotted leaders are essential to keep a looped-leader dry fly in place. You can, however, also use a knotless tapered leader with the looped-leader fly. Buy a 7½-foot tapered leader with a 3X tippet. Add a 30-inch piece of 4X fluorocarbon tippet to the 3X tippet. Connect the wet fly to the 4X tippet and place the looped-leader fly just above the knot. If you want to fish the wet fly deeper, add another piece of 4X or 5X fluorocarbon tippet to the 4X.

Tippets

Tippets, and the knots you use to connect them, can make or break a fishing trip. You want the finest, least visible leader with the strength you need to successfully land the biggest trout you hope to catch. I once invited a friend to a private fishing stream loaded with trout over 20 inches long. He'd been fly fishing for only a couple years and was unaccustomed to landing trout like this. He used a 3-pound-test tippet and broke off the first six trout. When he changed his tippet to 6-pound-test, he began landing trout. Why use a light leader and break off almost every trout you hook?

On the other hand, with today's pressured trout and advances in leader technology that have given us incredibly strong, thin-diameter tippets, it makes the most sense for me to generally fish 5X to 6X tippets, unless I am fishing streamers or large Green Drakes—or other similar wind-resistant dry flies. I can land most trout I catch swiftly with 4X and 5X tippet. On heavily fished streams, I often start with 6X or 7X tippets and 12- to 15-foot leaders.

I also recommend you use fluorocarbon tippets. For *How to Catch More Trout,* I conducted experiments where I used the same two patterns (a Patriot and a cream Glo Bug) with different leaders. Those tippets included 4X, 5X, and 6X regular and fluorocarbon. I often watched trout approach the Glo Bug and

Unpressured fish in wilderness rivers are easier to fool than fish on heavily pressured rivers, where you need to use fine tippets.

then turn away. The same trout often took the same pattern tied on 6X fluorocarbon tippet.

If you are just beginning to fish tandem rigs, you might want to sacrifice catching a few fish for your sanity. Use heavier tippets to start—such as 3X and 4X—to prevent tangles. These heavier tippets are fine with larger nymphs, streamers, and for fish that aren't as discerning, such as unpressured or stocked fish.

At first, space the flies no more than 12 to 16 inches apart. After you feel more confident casting two patterns, you can increase the distance. Use 4X tippet and a leader no longer than 7½ feet.

Fluorocarbon and Monofilament

I used to think tippet type didn't matter much, but I've changed my mind after a Montana fishing trip and a series of experiments. My son, Bryan, Ken Rictor, and Lynn Rotz accompanied me on the trip. Guided by Jerry Armstrong, we spent a day fishing some small ponds formed more than a century ago by gold-mining operations that had an abundant supply of cool spring water. Ken, Lynn, and Bryan headed off to other ponds while I remained at the largest one. In about an hour, they returned, dejected. Not one of them had a strike. When they asked how I had done, I told them I landed seven trout. We compared flies, tactics, and leaders and soon discovered that I was using fluorocarbon tippet while they were not. That was the only difference we could determine, so I added a fluorocarbon tippet to each of their leaders. Within minutes all three had trout on and within an hour caught ten trout among them.

I'm convinced that I catch more fish with fluorocarbon. To read more about my informal experiments, see *How to Catch More Trout*. Fluorocarbon is stronger than monofilament (but is generally less supple), so 4X to 6X tippets are exceptionally strong. The finer the tippet, the more you risk tangles and breaking off fish. But if trout seem to refuse your flies, switch to lighter tippet. On late-summer trips, I often start with 6X, and I sometimes use 7X to entice trout on heavily fished streams to take my flies.

Fluorocarbon is more expensive than monofilament, but if I catch three or four times as many trout, it's worth the price. Some knots good for monofilament are not as good for fluorocarbon—the improved clinch, for instance. Also fluorocarbon doesn't stretch as much as monofilament nylon, so it is more likely to break if a fish jerks. Though newer, improved fluorocarbons are still not as supple as the best mono, you compensate by reducing tippet size.

You don't need an entire leader made of fluorocarbon. I just tie on a fluorocarbon tippet to a monofilament leader, and I've seen no significant loss in strength from connecting the two different materials. Though fluorocarbon sinks, it shouldn't sink your indicator fly. Many people believe that the last bit of tippet should sink slightly and not float on the surface, where its reflection spooks fish.

Paul Weamer releases an early-season tandem-caught brown on the upper Delaware River, which is notorious for its difficult fish.

TECHNIQUES

In addition to leaders and tippets, two other factors (in addition to fly pattern) will help you catch more trout: drag-free drifts and fishing at the right depth.

Drag

Drag is the enemy of good presentation and occurs when the fly floats unnaturally. Varying currents often create troublesome drag, and trout usually won't take a fly that is not floating in synchrony with other objects on the surface.

Dead-Drift

One secret to catching more trout is a long drag-free float. Drag—more exactly, micro drag and the lack of it—separates expert from the novice. Follow something on the surface near your dry fly to determine whether it is floating like the objects unencumbered by tippet. If it isn't and a line mend won't correct it, then lift the flies out of the water and cast again. Trout can easily detect even the slightest drag. If mending alone doesn't do it, lengthen the leader or use finer tippet. If the dry fly is drifting drag-free on top, then you are probably getting a good drift with your wet fly. Bottom currents can flow slower than surface ones, so if the wet fly floats at a different speed than the dry fly, it can drag the dry fly and even pull it under.

In variable currents, I constantly mend line to obtain longer drag-free floats. One trick I use is called walking the dog. To get extended drifts, and if the streambank is relatively flat, I'll walk downstream at the speed of the fly's drift. You can even do this while wading as long as the currents aren't moving too fast or are too deep. Where you normally might get a 10- to 20-foot drag-free float mending the line, walking the dog can help extend it as far as you're able to walk.

Fly-fishing legend George Harvey uses the slack-leader cast to overcome drag. Harvey suggests that you aim the fly three or four feet above where you want it to land, stop the cast abruptly, then lower the fly rod so the fly lands on the water with a series of S-

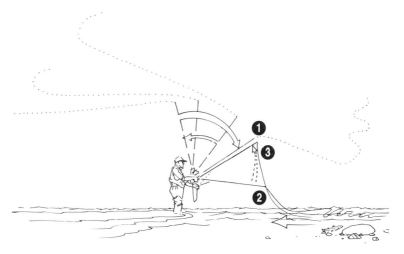

In the Harvey slack-leader cast, you (1) stop your rod high and (2) drop your arm to form S curves in the line. As the fly drifts back toward you, raise the rod tip (3).

curves in the leader (as long as the leader is built properly). As different currents pull on the leader, the S-curves uncurl, allowing the dry fly to float drag-free on the water until all the curves have straightened.

In faster water with varied currents, I constantly mend line to prevent drag by gently lifting the fly line upstream or downstream and making a loop in the fly line so the fly floats longer without drag. You should not violently yank the line and rip the fly out of the water or you'll scare all the trout in the area. If the water is faster near you and slower on the far shore, mend upstream; if the water nearer you is slower than the water where your fly is drifting, mend downstream. Make a series of short mends so you don't jerk the flies out of the water. One great benefit of fishing a dry-and-dropper rig is that you can often mend your fly line and leader easily without it affecting the drift of the submerged fly. The dry fly floating on the surface may twitch a little, but it acts like a shock absorber in the system.

If the water between you and the fish is faster than the water where your fly is, mend upstream for a longer drag-free float.

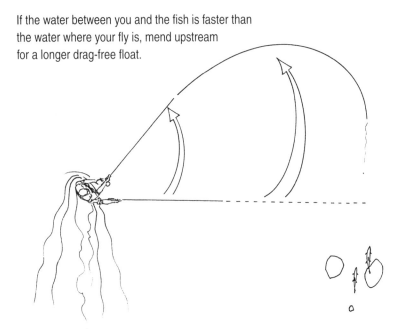

Active Presentations

Why do wet-fly anglers who cast across and downstream and let their patterns drag in an arc catch trout? That's how some insects emerge. Not all insects drift passively in the currents. As a mayfly emerges, it may actively swim toward the surface, not helplessly float in the current. Caddisflies often skitter along the surface when laying their eggs or emerging. To imitate this I often cast down and across and use line tension to help skitter my dry fly.

Eugene "Pooch" Delozier resides in Dunedin, Florida, but his heart lives in Pennsylvania. Pooch loves to fly fish, and when he returns to Pennsylvania he always fishes for trout. One day in mid-October I fished with Pooch, his son Garry, and his brother-in-law, Jim Slick. When I looked at Pooch's rig, I thought I was back in the 1940s. Pooch cast three snelled wet flies three quarters downstream. He would constantly move them, letting the flies drift for a second before gently lifting the rod tip, and then he'd repeat the technique until the flies were directly downstream of him. Pooch caught trout, so while I mainly preach a drag-free float, you can also move your flies. Which method is better? Let the fish decide.

This cutthroat took a Stimulator skittered across the surface. Heavily hackled downwing flies such as Elk-hair Caddis and Stimulators may attract fish by imitating some species of caddis and stoneflies that dance across the water as they emerge.

Depth

I can still remember talking to an old-timer more than thirty years ago on Bowman Creek in northeastern Pennsylvania. Even in late April I fished a dry fly, though no hatch appeared and no trout rose. The octogenarian watched me for a few minutes and then blurted out, "You won't catch anything on that dry fly—the trout aren't looking up yet. It's too early in the season." I never forgot those words of wisdom.

When you are determining how deep to set your dropper, consider the time of year you are fishing, where you are fishing, what you are fishing for, and whether insects are hatching. If you have confidence in your fly and leader, you're getting drifts without drag, and you're still not catching fish, change depth. Trout feed at different depths, and with multiple flies you can cover at least two levels at once. Whether trout are holding deep in icy water or you are fishing only a few inches beneath the surface to trout feeding on emerging *Callibaetis* just six to twelve inches under the surface of a lake, experiment to find a successful depth. Unless there's a hatch, I usu-

The depth at which you fish your fly is critical. Match the fly type (both indicator and nymph) with the depth you desire to fish. The larger the dry fly, the better it supports heavy nymphs that sink quickly to the bottom.

ally assume trout are feeding on or near bottom. In the cold water temperatures of early spring and late fall, I try to get the wet fly near the bottom. In the summer, I'll fish the entire water column because fish are often feeding closer to the surface.

The first time I fished for steelhead I was humbled. My son, Bryan, and his buddies Bill Magliore, Tom Hutchison, Eric Melby, and I fished for an entire day on Eighteenmile Creek in Hamburg, New York, and I never had a strike. Three years later, I returned, determined to catch a steelhead. When I first fished it, Eighteenmile ran high and fast. Now it was low and clear.

This second trip was special. The next day, Bryan was to marry Julie Light in a church a few miles from the stream. He had invited some friends and members of his wedding party—Eric Melby, Austin Morrow, and Bill Magliore—to fish before the wedding. A fresh run of steelhead had entered the stream, and we all fished in great anticipation. All of Bryan's buddies used one fly with a poly strike indicator. I, on the other hand, used a Patriot and a weighted cream Glo Bug. I tied on 60 inches of tippet between the dry and wet flies. The weighted fly and the increased distance between the two flies helped me get to the bottom, exactly where I should be.

Within minutes, Bryan hooked and landed a fresh six-pounder. For more than an hour, I fished without a strike. Déjà vu. I thought more and more about the foiled fishing trip three years ago. By the second hour, I got anxious—no, frustrated. I could sense Bryan was also concerned that I'd be shut out again. Then, the Patriot sank, and I set the hook. Thirty feet away and off to my right side, a heavy steelhead erupted. It jumped two more times before I beached the fresh six-

Charles Meck (left) and son, Bryan, on New York's Eighteenmile Creek.

pounder. Now the snide was off my back, and I could relax and enjoy the fishing, friends, and stream.

I continued to fish a deep riffle at the head of the pool, and within minutes the dry fly sank again. I set the hook, and a heavy fish came completely out of the water between me and the shore showing itself five times in fifteen minutes before I finally beached it. Bryan estimated that it weighed about twelve pounds. Not bad for that second trip.

Weight

Weight makes all the difference in the world, and you can sink your flies in different ways: add weight to your fly, fish a streamlined fly

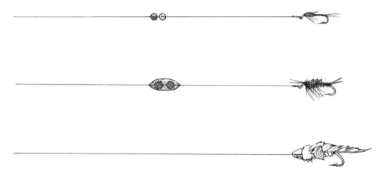

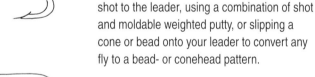

Above: You can sink your fly by adding split-shot to the leader, using a combination of shot and moldable weighted putty, or slipping a cone or bead onto your leader to convert any fly to a bead- or conehead pattern.

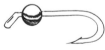

Left: I prefer to weight my flies instead of adding weight to the leader, though sometimes you have to do both. You can weight your flies with (from top to bottom) lead or lead-alternative wire, beads, cones, or weighted dumbbell eyes (not shown).

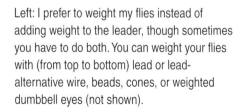

such as a Zebra Midge or Brassie, use a weighted fly such as a Copper John to sink your rig, or add weight to the leader. I prefer to add weight to the fly at the vise or fish flies with beads tied into them.

You can also add lead shot to your leader. If you are fishing all nymphs, you can add shot above the first nymph and between the nymphs. If you are fishing a dry and a dropper, you can add split-shot between the dry and dropper. Be cautious with adding weight to your tippets, however. Larger split-shot tends to twist and tangle the line. Micro shot is great for adding to the leader on nymphs that are fished below dry flies because it is small and you can slowly add weight until you reach your desired depth.

Lead putty is also handy because you can add it or take it away as needed. Many anglers use a combination of micro shot and lead putty and form the putty around the micro shot or around the last knot on their leader before the wet fly. Experiment with the amount of weight you can use and still keep your dry fly floating.

Adding too much weight to your dropper nymph can quickly sink the dry fly. On smaller patterns, flies tied on size 18 or 20 scud

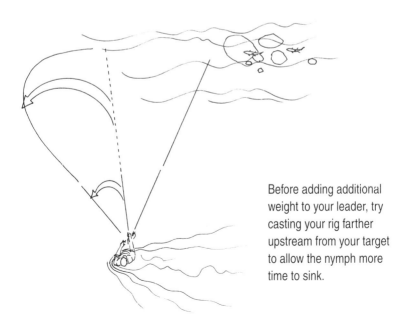

Before adding additional weight to your leader, try casting your rig farther upstream from your target to allow the nymph more time to sink.

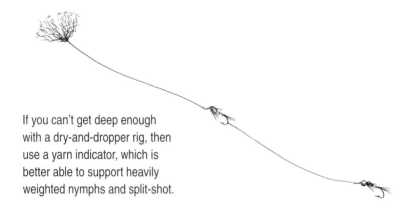

If you can't get deep enough with a dry-and-dropper rig, then use a yarn indicator, which is better able to support heavily weighted nymphs and split-shot.

hooks, you can add a tungsten bead. But, large flies with tungsten beads or too much lead shot can sink some dry flies. If you want to fish heavy nymphs, use large, foam or deer-hair dry flies such as B/C Hoppers, Chernobyls, Turck Tarantulas, and large stonefly patterns.

Casting Techniques

In 1989, Don Whitesel illustrated *Pennsylvania Trout Streams and Their Hatches* for me. Shortly after the book was published, Don and I fished together. I tied on a Patriot and a Beadhead Pheasant Tail for Don. On the first cast he stopped his false-cast abruptly and tangled the tandem—it was at least a half-hour, maybe even an hour, tangle. We should have cut off the leader and started over, it was such a mess.

I showed slides of that tangle at a presentation in Denver, Colorado. Then I showed a slide of the next cast after Don untangled the leader and the two flies. On that cast, Don had a strike on the wet fly, set the hook, and landed a fat three-pound brown trout. On the cast after that, he caught that first trout's twin. Don's luck changed instantly. An angler in the audience raised his hand and said that it must have taken a long time to untangle the line. The slide of the tangled line was taken in complete daylight; the slide showing that first heavy brown was taken with a flash.

Even experienced casters get occasional tangles. Here are some tips to reduce the amount of bird's-nest tangles you get in your line.

Keep false-casting to a minimum. False-cast only as much as it takes you to dry the lead fly (if it's a dry fly). Often, one or two false-casts are all you need. If your fly is waterlogged, then use dessicant or an amadou patch to dry it. The more false-casts, the more tangles. If you are fishing all wet flies, do not false-cast at all.

Slow down your casting stroke. Anglers casting multiple flies for the first time tend to have trouble with timing. Wait until your back cast has almost straightened before you begin your forward cast.

Cast open loops. When you cast more than one fly at a time, cast wider loops. Keep those six-inch loops for when you are casting one dry fly. Make certain that you have a smooth stroke with a fairly open loop to prevent heavier flies from catching your leader on your false-casts.

Use the Belgian cast. Instead of casting in a single plane, you should cast the flies around in a circle to prevent tangles when fishing more than one fly, whether you are fishing dry flies, dry and dropper, or multiple streamers. Begin your backcast sidearm, but come forward with a standard overhead cast. Pulling the line around in a oval like this prevents the line from hitting itself and tangling.

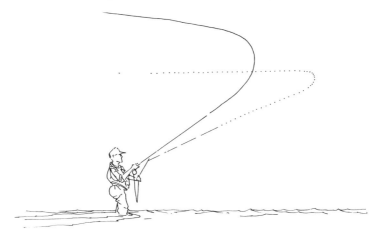

When you are fishing multiple flies, cast wider loops than you would if you were fishing a single dry fly. You lob weighted nymphs and double streamers more than you cast them.

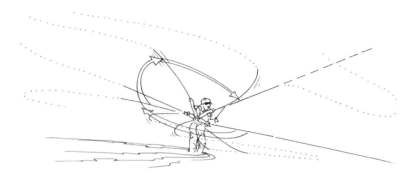

The Belgian cast (sometimes called the oval cast) is an effective way to cast multiple-fly rigs, weighted flies, and sinking lines. Begin the backcast sidearm and come forward over your head.

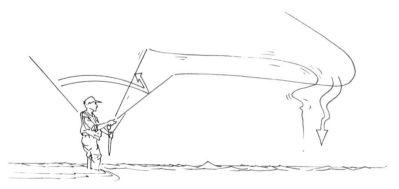

The parachute cast helps sink your nymphs faster and can be used in combination with the Belgian cast. Aim the last forward cast about twenty feet high. I stop the leader short and let the entire rig fall to the surface. If you make this cast with a weighted wet fly, the wet enters the water first and sinks quickly.

Learn the parachute cast. This cast helps sink your nymphs faster and can be used in combination with the Belgian cast. Aim the last forward cast about twenty feet high, stop the rod tip, and let the entire rig fall to the surface. If you make this cast with a weighted wet fly, the wet enters the water first and sinks quickly. The one disadvantage with this method is that you get fewer S-curves in your leader and the dry fly drags more quickly.

Don't get discouraged by the first tangle. You'll have a fair share of tangles and frustrations, but the rewards from using the tandem far outweigh its shortfalls. Don't waste valuable fishing time trying to untangle your line. Sometimes it is faster to cut the line and rerig.

Always check your flies. I'll never forget the time Dave Tongue handed my fly rod back to me and complained that he hadn't had a strike. I began casting and casting and casting—and no strikes. Finally, after forty or more good drifts without a strike, I checked the rig: the Zebra Midge tangled with my dry fly, and there was no way a trout could have hit either. After that, I faithfully check my rig every few minutes.

Setting the Hook

If the dry fly hesitates, I set the hook, but sometimes that's not quick enough. Often by the time you react to a strike on the dry fly or movement of the indicator, the fish has struck the wet fly and veered away. I try to watch the dry fly and the wet at the same time and strike if I see a fish flash or white mouth near where I think my wet fly is. If you have too much slack fly line on the water, you can't set the hook quickly.

STRATEGIES FOR SPECIAL CIRCUMSTANCES
Lakes and Ponds

My son, Bryan, and I fished a small spring-fed pond near Alder, Montana. A heavy crop of aquatic weeds grew from the bottom of the pond to within two feet of the surface. You could not fish wet flies unless you suspended them from a dry fly or strike indicator. That afternoon no one caught trout—that is, until Bryan tied a wet fly 20 inches behind the dry fly so that the wet fly drifted just above the weeds. On the first cast a trout hit. On the second cast, a trout hit again. When no one else caught fish, Bryan landed more than twenty. The other anglers crowded around Bryan to see what he did differently. That evening, Bryan and I tied flies and set up tandem rigs for all the guests. The next day, many of the anglers caught fish with the new rigs.

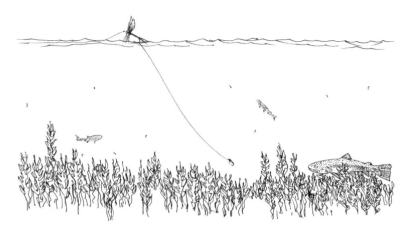

A dry-and-dropper rig allows you to suspend your nymph over obstructions or at the level fish are feeding and is an effective tactic when fishing weedbeds in lakes.

Depth is critical in lakes and ponds, so experiment to find where trout are feeding. The right flies at the right depth can pay off big.

Sometimes trout would rather hit a moving fly and when you're fishing a wet fly under a dry, you might have to twitch it to entice fish. When fishing stillwaters, wind and waves often combine to impart motion to a wet fly by moving the dry fly or strike indicator connected to it. If trout are really keying on a moving fly, then you may fish two wets or two streamers with strips and forgo the indicator.

Good subsurface flies for stillwaters include chironomids, midge larvae and pupae, damselfly nymphs, and *Callibaetis* nymphs. Indicator flies make fishing small midges a snap.

Depth is critical in lakes and ponds, so experiment to find the depth at which the trout are feeding.

Small Streams

The tandem takes a lot of the guesswork out of fishing smaller streams. June through August I often fish ant and beetle patterns on smaller streams. These and other small, dark terrestrials are often difficult to follow on waters with heavy, shading canopy. That's where the tandem comes in handy. Tie your small terrestrial on 12 to 18 inches of tippet behind an easy-to-see pattern like a Patriot or Trout Fin and follow the dry fly to estimate the terrestrial's location. When a fish takes a small ant or beetle, the takes are often only small rings, so you still need to pay attention. If you really want to clean up, fish a weighted ant, beetle, or cricket behind a dry fly.

Low Water

Travis Robison invited me to fish for a day on Wills Creek near Somerset, Pennsylvania. I trashed Wills Creek in *Pennsylvania Trout Streams and Their Hatches* and said it wasn't worth fishing. At that time, the stream held few trout through the hot summer months

On small streams, try fishing a beetle or ant behind an easy-to-see dry like a Humpy, Patriot, Royal Wulff, or Stimulator.

and was still recovering from a flood. Travis felt that the stream had come a long way since the late 1980s, and he invited me back seventeen years later to show me.

In early August, we met in Hydman and headed to the stream. When we approached the water, it was only a trickle, and Robison apologized for the conditions, saying that the stream was a shadow of itself in April. Huge boulders baked in the sun where just a few months before they were almost covered with water. But Wills Creek's one salvation is its drop in elevation. In just ten miles the stream plummets 1,300 feet. This drop creates deep pools—some four to eight feet deep—even in a drought.

The first pool we approached held a few large trout that scattered the minute we got within twenty feet of the pool. As we headed upstream and attempted to fish each of the pools, trout fled. In addition to the low water, these fish also experienced heavy angling pressure, which made them incredibly wary. On the way up the stream we counted more than ten cars with fishermen in them; and remember, this was in early August, which isn't exactly fly-fishing prime time in Pennsylvania.

We fished for two hours. Though many trout swirled at our flies, we caught nothing. Travis and I sat back and began to reconsider our strategies. I decided to fish smaller flies and finer tippet. I replaced my size 12 Patriot with a size 14, then tied a size 16 Glo Bug to the bend with 6X fluorocarbon. If reducing fly size and tippet didn't work, I planned to try a different pattern.

Travis fished the pool with a March Brown dry and a Green Weenie. We saw six fish in the pool, and not one looked at the fly. I was up next. I crept up to the stream, well downstream from the fish so I didn't scare them. On the second cast, the Patriot sank and I set the hook. A large fish was on for a split second before it broke off. It was a shame to lose the fish, but I felt good knowing that I was able to fool it despite the tough conditions. When fishing in low water, remember these three things: use the finest fluorocarbon tippet you feel comfortable with, cast as far away from the fish as possible and keep a low profile, and use smaller flies if larger ones scare the fish.

High, Cloudy Waters

The summer of 2004 seemed like a carbon copy of 2003. May through August, heavy rains inundated New York, New Jersey, Maryland, and Pennsylvania. Trout streams ran bank-full. But the weather should have been the least of my worries. In early May I broke my left arm (my writing arm) when I fell off a ladder. Pins put in the arm became infected, and I suffered for much of the summer with excruciating pains. I couldn't fish for three months.

But, that didn't stop me from accompanying friends and playing "guide." Many of those trips were almost wasted because of high water, and we probably should have cancelled several of them. But because we did fish and catch trout, the valuable lessons we learned are worth passing along.

You'll often encounter less-than-favorable stream conditions. In high, cloudy water, you need to modify your rig by fishing at least one brightly colored fly, adjust the depth at which you fish, and focus on fishing your fly in backeddies and other spots in the stream where currents are slower than the main flow. In high, flooded waters, look for backwaters and eddies where trout station out of the faster water to feed. If you don't catch trout in these areas, fish your fly on the bottom through some of the regular spots.

In high water, large, bright subsurface patterns such as Mickey Finns, chartreuse Clouser Minnows, Royal Coachmans, and Green Weenies work well. Pink is a deadly color, and

Whether fishing low, clear water or high, cloudy waters you can modify your tandem rig to help you catch more fish. The author rigs a tandem on Bald Eagle Creek, Pennsylvania, 2007.

a fly called the Pink Ugly (a large pink streamer I first saw tied by Ron German's wife, Flossie, who was from Smethport, Pennsylvania) works extremely well in high, dirty water.

Recently, Fred Bridge of York, Pennsylvania, gave me a pattern he calls the Pink Worm, which is nothing more than an orange dubbed body of angora yarn with a piece of bright pink vernille tied over top and extended an inch beyond the eye and the hook bend. One day, in poor fishing conditions, I handed one of these to Bill Sharpe and his son, Peter. Bill and Peter didn't do well until they got the Pink Worm on or within a few inches of the bottom by adding two light lead shot to the leader six inches above the fly, but when they did, the two caught fifteen trout.

When I fish a heavily weighted wet fly in high water, I use a large poly strike indicator, which floats under even the most adverse conditions. In high water, I have no problem giving up on the dry-fly strike indicator because few fish will probably strike it.

One day in high water (two feet above the stream's normal flow) I decided to test the effectiveness of the tandem. I tied on a Green Weenie with twenty wraps of .010-inch-diameter lead under a Patriot. Another angler, Mike Berwager, stopped by to watch. He wasn't fishing because of the conditions but wanted to see how well I did. In the first half-hour I didn't have a strike and was just about ready to quit.

I moved to a slower section and cast the same two patterns. On the second cast, the dry fly sank, and I set the hook. A 10-inch brown trout jumped out of the cloudy water two times before I landed it. After two more casts in the slower water, I landed another brown, slightly larger than the first. I picked up seven trout before I switched to a red version of the Green Weenie, called the I'm Not Sure.

CHAPTER 7

Fishing the Hatches

When there's a hatch, I like to match it. My strategy when fishing two flies is to use a dry fly that copies the dun and a wet fly that looks like the nymph or emerger. I call this rig the bi-cycle because it imitates two stages of the emerging insect. You can also try a dry fly, emerger, and nymph—a rig I call the tri-cycle—but three flies takes more practice to cast than two.

The bi-cycle approach is important because it helps you cover several bases at once. In late-August 1999, my son, Bryan, and I

When there's a hatch, I like to match it, but sometimes it is hard to figure out exactly what the fish are feeding on.

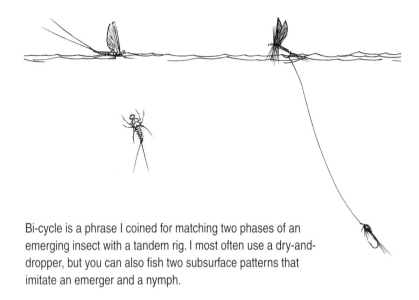

Bi-cycle is a phrase I coined for matching two phases of an emerging insect with a tandem rig. I most often use a dry-and-dropper, but you can also fish two subsurface patterns that imitate an emerger and a nymph.

fished southcentral Pennsylvania's Yellow Breeches Creek. Around that time every year, the White Fly, one of the season's last great hatches, emerges for more than two weeks. The insects begin emerging around 7:30 P.M. and often continue hatching after dark.

Anglers crowded in on us as the intense hatch began to pick up steam. There were so many anglers, it was like opening day. Bryan and I caught a dozen trout on the pair of flies we were fishing— White Fly dry flies with pale-gray White Fly nymphs two feet below them—which is an accomplishment, at least for me, with the intense fishing pressure. I caught nine trout on the nymph and three on the dry. That night, the fish seemed to be feeding more heavily on the nymphs and emergers.

MAYFLIES

A year after a mayfly egg is fertilized, the nymph transforms near the bottom and begins to move toward the surface or swim to shore or an exposed object to hatch. At the bottom, or near the water's surface, the nymph (now also called an emerger) splits its skin and appears on the surface as a mayfly dun, usually an immature, non-mating adult. Some mayfly species, such as Quill Gordons, emerge on the bottom; some, such as Gray and Slate Drakes swim to shore; and others, such as March Browns, emerge near the surface.

The chart on pages 82–83 lists common mayflies and where in the stream they emerge. Knowing the location and depth at which an insect emerges helps you determine how deep and in what manner to fish your subsurface flies. Most anglers fish all their emerger patterns near the surface, but many mayflies swim to shore or change from nymph to dun at or near the bottom. This means you should fish bottom emergers deep and copy mayfly nymphs that swim to shore or to an exposed rock by moving or twitching your fly.

Changing from underwater insect to an air-breathing one often takes time. This emerger stage is the most vulnerable in the mayfly's life cycle (the phase where the spinner falls spent on the surface is equally important—but, in this stage there is less food value). Trout sense the emergers are defenseless and readily feed on them. The first part of the dun to show through is the wing and

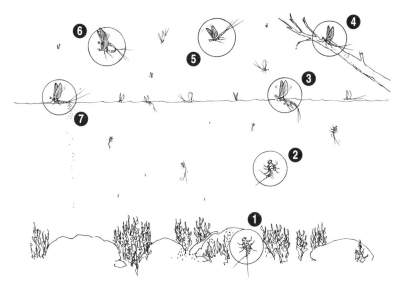

Mayfly life cycle. Mayfly nymph (1) swims to the surface to emerge (2, 3) then flies to streamside vegetation where it molts (4) into a sexually mature adult (5) and mates (6). Females return to the water to lay eggs (7). Note: not all mayflies emerge in this manner. See chart on pages 82–83.

head area. From the moment the shuck splits until the dun emerges, the mayfly is completely defenseless. I am convinced that the trout often search out this phase.

In two hours to a day or more after it emerges, the dun changes again. It loses its outer skin and becomes a spinner with glassy, clear wings, and a mating adult. Often, in the evening, male spinners swarm over or near the water waiting for females to join them. When the female spinners enter the swarm, the males impregnate them, and the females then move toward the water's surface to deposit their fertilized eggs. Female spinners often fall to the surface after laying their eggs. Many of these spent females sink under the surface. Also, some species dive under the surface to lay their eggs.

I often sit back and watch before I fish. One cloudy, misty late-May afternoon on a central Pennsylvania river I watched four insects hatch simultaneously. In front of me more than fifty trout fed on the smorgasbord of Little Blue-Winged Olives, Green Drakes, Slate Drakes, and Sulphurs. In the midst of all of this, I sat and watched, trying to determine what the trout were keying on. Most of the risers seemed to be taking the Sulphur. A few took the dun, but many of the "rises" were really swirls just under the surface. In several instances I saw trout miss the emerger, and I watched the dun take off just above the swirl. I tied on a size 16 long-shank Sulphur Emerger two feet behind a size 12 Patriot, and for more than two hours that afternoon caught lots of trout on the emerger.

You should know the approximate times the different hatches appear. You don't have to memorize the hatches, just be aware that if cream is the predominant color of mayflies emerging on summer evenings then you should use emergers with cream heads; if Sulphurs are hatching, use emergers with yellowish-orange heads.

Fishing an emerger under an attractor pattern or a pattern that copies the dun works before, during, and after the hatch. You don't have to fish an emerger just under the water's surface. Emergers can be effective (and sometimes most effective) fished on the bottom like a nymph. I learned this lesson watching Jeff Blood high-stick nymph a Sulphur emerger while filming an episode of *The New Fly*

Fisher, hosted by Colin McKeown. Even though the fishing that day was poor overall—high water, no hatches—Jeff Blood caught lots of fish with a version of the Universal Emerger.

**Universal Emerger
(Pale Morning Dun
and Sulphur)**

Hook:	Size 12-16 Mustad 3906B or equivalent
Thread:	6/0 pale yellow
Tail:	Five pheasant-tail fibers
Body:	Pheasant-tail fibers ribbed with fine gold wire
Thorax:	Fluffy feathers at the base of the pheasant-tail feather or hackle
Head:	Tying thread

Adjust the thorax color to imitate various species. From April to early May, use a #12-16 pattern with gray or tan head; mornings from late May to late August use a #12-16 pattern with a gray or olive head; evenings from late May to late August use a #12-16 pattern with a cream, yellow, gray, or brown head; and September and later use a #12-18 pattern with a gray or olive head.

This relatively simple system reflects the way that I like to simplify the mayfly hatches. Early and late in the season, the bugs are dark; in the summer, they are light (but generally only the evening emergers). More specifically, in the spring, mayfly duns are grays and browns; summer mornings, grays and olives; summer evenings, yellow, cream and a few brown and grays; and after September, grays and olives. The thorax (or head) color of the Universal Emerger matches the dun's body color.

Spring grays generally emerge early to mid-afternoon, spring tans and browns in the afternoon, late spring and summer creams

MAYFLIES AND EMERGENCE LOCATION

Name	Range	Emerges
Spring Grays		
Blue Quill (*Paraleptophlebia adoptiva*) #18	E, M	S
Dark Olive (*Siphloplecton basale*) #12	E	T
Quill Gordon (*Epeorus pleuralis*) #14	E	B
Blue-Winged Olive (*Baetis tricaudatus*) #20	all	B
Black Quill (*Leptophlebia cupida*) #12	E, M	S
Spring Tan and Browns		
Hendrickson (*Ephemerella subvaria*) #14	E, M	B
W. March Brown (*Rhithrogena morrisoni*) #14	W	T
Late Spring and Summer Creams		
March Brown (*Maccaffertium vicarium*) #12	E, M	T
Light Cahill (*Stenacron interpunctatum*) #14	E, M	T
Pale Morning Dun (*Ephemerella excrucians, E. dorothea infrequens*) #16-18	W	T, M
Sulphur (*Ephemerella rotunda, E. dorothea dorothea*) #16-18	E, M	T, M
Green Drake (*Ephemera guttulata*) #10	E	T
Yellow Drake (*Ephemera varia*) #12	E, M	T
Golden Drake (*Anthopotamus distinctus*) #12	E, M	T
Gray Fox (*Heptagenia solitaria*) #14	W	T
Pink Lady (*Epeorus albertae*) #14	W	B
White Fly (*Ephoron leukon, E. album*) #14	all	T
Green Drake (*Hexagenia rigida*) #6	E	T

Where Found: E=East, M=Midwest, W=West, All=all areas of the United States
Emerges: S=swims to shore or exposed debris to emerge, B=emerges near bottom,
T=emerges near surface, M=emerges near the middle to the surface

MAYFLIES AND EMERGENCE LOCATION *continued*

Name	Range	Emerges
Late Spring and Summer Olives and Grays (morning)		
BWO (*Drunella sp.*) #14	all	B
W. Green Drake (*Drunella grandis*) #12	W	B
Blue Quill (*Paraleptophlebia mollis*) #18	E, M	S
Speckle-winged Dun (*Callibaetis americanus*) #14	W	T
Gray Drake (*Siphlonurus* sp.) #12	all	S
Trico (*Tricorythodes* sp.) #24	all	S, B
Summer Darks (evening)		
Slate Drake (*Isonychia bicolor*) #12	E, M	S
Brown Drake (*Ephemera simulans*) #12	all	T
Hex (*Hexagenia limbata*) #8	M, W	T
Fall Grays		
Slate Drake (*Isonychia bicolor*) #14	E, M	S
BWO (*Baetis tricaudatus*) #20	all	B
Blue Quills (*Paraleptophlebia guttata*) #18	E, M	S

Where Found: E=East, M=Midwest, W=West, All=all areas of the United States
Emerges: S=swims to shore or exposed debris to emerge, B=emerges near bottom,
T=emerges near surface, M=emerges near the middle to the surface

generally late afternoon to evening, late spring and summer olives
and grays hatch in the morning, dark summer flies hatch in the
evening, and fall insects hatch in the afternoons, with the exception
of some fall Paraleps species, which hatch in the morning. All hatch
times are influenced by water temperatures, so spring creeks and
tailwaters can have different hatch times than those listed, as can
inordinately warm freestone streams. These emergence times are
just guidelines.

STONEFLIES AND CADDISFLIES

Anglers often call caddisflies and stoneflies downwings because their resting wings lie along their bodies. Small Golden Stone and Yellow Sally nymphs and caddis pupae and larvae are popular flies to fish in tandem rigs. Both caddis and stonefly adult imitations make excellent, and some of the most popular, indicator flies. Common caddis rigs are CDC and Elks, Elk-Hair Caddis, or Goddard Caddis and a mayfly nymph such as a Pheasant Tail or Copper John. Stonefly dries make excellent indicator flies and can float several flies or one heavily weighted pattern. Understanding the life cycles of caddis and stoneflies will help you determine when fishing these patterns is the best choice.

Caddisflies

Caddisflies lack tough exoskeletons, so some species (but not all) construct a protective shelter or case. Some caddis, like the Green Caddis (*Rhyacophila*), are free living on the bottom and construct no shelter. Other important caddis, like the Grannom (*Brachycentrus*), build twig cases. Still others build nets (Little Black Caddis and Dark Blue Sedge (*Psilotreta*) or cases of coarse stone fragments. The larvae turn into pupae inside their cases. You can often predict the predominate species in a stream by the material that's available for the larvae to use for cases.

Two of my favorite subsurface patterns to imitate caddis are the Beadhead Tan Caddis (imitates *Symphitopsyche*, formerly *Hydropsyche*) and the Beadhead Olive Caddis (imitates *Rhyacophila*). Both have saved me on many trips in the past decade. I fish the caddis patterns with both a dead-drift and a twitch, especially during a hatch.

Stoneflies

Stonefly nymphs take one to three years to develop, depending on the species. Therefore, in a stream with Salmonflies, for instance, fish see and feed on different sizes because that particular species takes three years to complete its life cycle. When you imitate the nymph, you can use a range of sizes, and you don't always have to use the largest. This is important, because dry-and-dropper rigs have to be balanced—the nymph should not be too heavy for the dry fly that you've chosen to support it.

Because nymphs and larvae are available to trout almost every day of the year (whereas adults are available for only a few days), stonefly nymphs are always good subsurface patterns. Stonefly nymphs live on underwater rocks. When they're ready to emerge, most nymphs swim to an exposed rock or to shore and fish look for migrating stoneflies in shallower water. Large Salmonfly imitations such as Kaufmann Stones or black Woolly Buggers are often so heavy that an indicator fly is impractical, and they are best fished under an indicator. However, you can fish imitations of the smaller stoneflies such as Yellow Sallies and early-season black stoneflies under an indicator fly with great results.

Adult caddis and stonefly imitations make excellent indicator flies. A yellow Stimulator is an effective, high-floating indicator fly that catches trout across the country. Depending on the size, it can represent Yellow Sallies, Golden Stones, or grasshoppers, all common on trout streams across the United States. For fishing rivers

Stonefly nymphs live in most trout streams with well-oxygenated water. They are great choices for subsurface flies in a tandem rig. This upper Delaware brown preferred a Golden Stone nymph pattern over the mayfly imitation trailing behind it.

Foam and deer-hair stonefly patterns can also represent hoppers.

with faster currents for fish that are accustomed to larger foods (or see less pressure) such as some Western waters, flies such as Chernobyl Ants, Turck's Tarantulas, and foam-bodied stoneflies hold up well and float high on fast rivers and streams. To make the patterns more visible, add a bright piece of orange, yellow, or white poly on top of the wing.

MIDGES

Midges are important because they live in almost every body of water that holds trout, and fish feed on them year-round. On many streams, midges are the main game for trout. Though small, they are an abundant and dependable food source. Trout open their mouths wide and filter feed on midges like whales feed on krill.

Streams like Pennsylvania's Yellow Breeches or Spring Creek (near State College) or the San Juan in New Mexico or Frying Pan in Colorado are midge factories, and anglers that have frequent and consistent success on these streams and rivers—and others like them—have learned how to effectively fish small flies.

Small patterns that imitate midge larvae and pupae, such as the Zebra Midge, Craven's Jujubee Midge, Barr's Pure Midge, or Brassie are perfectly suited for the tandem because, at least for me, they are nearly impossible to fish effectively any other way, except for maybe under a strike indicator. While you wouldn't expect a trout to eat your dry fly in the dead of winter, it often helps to have an indicator fly. Carry black, olive, and red patterns to match the most common larvae. Change the length of your dropper to suspend the midge at the exact depth that the fish are feeding. Instead of waiting for the dry fly to twitch, watch for the trout's white mouth or flash of movement as it takes the fly—and set the hook. To imitate adult midges, it's hard to beat the simplicity of a Griffith's Gnat trailed behind an easy-to-see indicator fly.

This brown took a small midge pupa drifting behind a size 18 *Baetis* imitation.

CHAPTER 8

Dry Fly Patterns

The dry fly in a dry-and-dropper rig should be easy to see, float well, and catch trout. Most of the time, I prefer to use a size 12 Patriot as the "strike indicator." I can easily detect its white wings on the surface, and tied on a light-wire hook with plenty of stiff hackle, it floats almost any small to medium wet fly. The Stimulator and hopper patterns I list carry a heavier load and are important when fishing heavy nymphs in deep or fast water. All of these dry flies are good for non-hatch periods. And some, like Ken's Hopper, Hybrid, and Trout Fin, are good hatch-matchers. Your pattern preference may vary from foam flies with rubber legs to slimmer Parachutes. They all have a time and place, depending on the water type you are fishing, the profile of any adult insect activity at the time, and the fly's ability to suspend the subsurface fly or flies you want to fish.

PATRIOT

I first tied the Patriot in 1985 after reading an article in *Flyfishing the West* about two scientists from British Columbia who studied the color of steelhead eggs rainbow trout preferred. The scientists concluded that the rainbows often preferred blue, even though there are no blue eggs in nature.

My first version of the Patriot had a blue marabou body ribbed with red floss, and I called it the RB (Really Blue) Coachman. I caught plenty of trout with it, but the marabou body absorbed water quickly and sank. When Krystal Flash came on the market, I tied a few RBs with smolt-blue bodies ribbed with bright orange-red tying thread. The pattern looked great and caught a lot more trout. I can still remember fishing one of the prototypes on the Youghiogheny River in 1989 with Art Gusbar of Somerset, Pennsylvania. I caught two trout on the pattern and Art wanted to look at it. He immediately named it the Patriot because of its red midrib, white wings, and blue body.

For my needs, the Patriot is a great all-purpose indicator fly, but it will not float large nymphs like stoneflies or Woolly Buggers or multiple heavy nymphs. Though I most often fish it in a size 12, I'll go down to a size 16 or 18 when fishing it as an indicator fly for a Trico spinner.

Patriot

Hook:	Size 12-18 dry fly
Thread:	6/0 bright orange-red
Tail:	Brown hackle fibers
Body:	Smolt-blue Krystal Flash with a midrib of red tying thread
Hackle:	Brown
Wings:	White calf-body hair

HYBRID

The Hybrid combines what I feel are the best attributes of the Adams and the Gray and Ausable Wulffs. It has the Ausable Wulff's highly visible wings, the Adams' brown and grizzly hackle, and the gray body of both the Adams and Gray Wulff. The gray body works especially well when grayish early- and late-season mayflies hatch.

It works well throughout the year, but I most often use it during spring and fall. I first tested the Hybrid on the upper Delaware in September when the Slate Drakes (*Isonychia*) were hatching and did well with the pattern. I use size 18s to match the small Blue Quills and *Baetis*.

Hybrid

Hook:	Size 12-18 dry fly
Thread:	6/0 gray
Tail:	Tan deer hair
Body:	Medium- to dark-gray synthetic dubbing
Hackle:	Brown and grizzly, or cree
Wings:	White calf-body hair

TROUT FIN

Forty years ago, I first watched John Weaver, an angler from the Wilkes-Barre, Pennsylvania area, cast two Trout Fins together on Bowman Creek. Sometimes John caught two trout on the same cast, and when he caught a double and the line would tangle, he'd sometimes work on untangling his leader for up to a half-hour. Every evening—all summer long—John caught trout on that bright orange fly.

I finally tried a Trout Fin one late June evening on Bowman Creek. It worked, and I caught trout when no hatch appeared, and when the water level was extremely low. After that, the Trout Fin had a permanent home in my box. More than a pretty attractor, the fly also copies the orange-bodied mayflies prevalent June through August.

The Trout Fin works as well today as it did then. I conducted a test of twenty dry flies including an Adams, Light Cahill, Royal

Wulff, Royal Coachman, March Brown, Patriot, and Trout Fin on the Little Juniata River. I cast each dry fly one thousand times over water where no trout rose and over a period of two months. I had a counter and kept an accurate record of the number of casts. Wow! I made fishing tedious for those two months. Of the twenty patterns I tested when no trout rose, the Trout Fin came in as second best behind the Patriot—even better than the venerable Adams or Wulff.

In the 1960s, before synthetic materials, John used orange silk for the Trout Fin's body, but over the years I have opted for bright orange poly yarn, which floats better and doesn't change color like silk. John used white quill sections for the wings, but they spin and twist, so I switched to white calf-body hair.

Trout Fin

Hook:	Size 12-18 dry fly
Thread:	6/0 orange
Tail:	Furnace hackle fibers
Body:	Bright orange poly yarn or orange poly dubbing
Hackle:	Furnace
Wings:	White calf-body hair

WHITE-WINGED BLUEBIRD

The White-Winged Bluebird is one of the best and easiest-to-see patterns that I've come up with in years. I dye cream hackle with evening-blue Rit dye until I get a rich, light- to medium-blue shade. The White-Winged Bluebird not only has a bright blue body but also a blue tail and legs and easy-to-follow white wing. When nothing else works—even wet flies—trout often take this fly on the surface with a vengeance. This pattern works especially well for brook trout on my favorite haunts—overlooked small streams.

White-Winged Bluebird

Hook: Size 12-14 dry fly
Thread: 6/0 medium blue
Tail: Evening-blue dyed hackle fibers
Body: Smolt-blue Krystal Flash with a red midrib
Hackle: Evening-blue dyed hackle
Wings: White calf-body hair

KEN'S HOPPER

Ken's Hopper is an excellent dry in a hopper-dropper combination. Use the hopper pattern in the summer and when you encounter high water. Though it is not as elaborate as some other hopper imitations, it is quick, easy to tie, and easy to see.

This fly is named after the late and great Ken Sink of Indiana, Pennsylvania. One day, in the 1970s, Ken landed more than thirty heavy trout on one of his hopper patterns on a central Pennsylvania stream. On his last cast of the day, Ken snagged his fly high in a nearby pine tree. It was his last one, and he forgot exactly how he tied the fly. He had to get it back intact. He jiggled and yanked for nearly a half-hour without freeing the treasure. Finally the leader came back without the fly, the hopper dangling high up in the tree with a small piece of leader trailing behind it.

The next day, Ken invited me to fish with him at that same spot. It was more than just a friendly invitation. Ken hauled an extension ladder out of the back of his truck. When we got to the creek he placed it up against the tree with his hopper in it and asked me to climb up and get his fly back. I reluctantly agreed and finally freed the fly from a branch. That fly must have been good to Ken for him to go through all of that work. It still works well for me.

Ken's Hopper

Hook: Size 8-12 long-shank
dry fly
Thread: 6/0 yellow
Body: Yellowish olive, olive,
or yellow poly
Head and wings:
Deer body hair dyed
yellow

CONVERTIBLE STIMULATOR

Like hoppers, Stimulators also make fantastic indicator flies, especially if you encounter high, deep, or fast water. The Convertible Stimulator is one of my favorite flies, and its yellow body copies many larger mayflies, caddisflies, stoneflies, and terrestrials, which is why I call it the Convertible Stimulator. You can even pull it under the water and fish it like a Muddler. The fly floats like a bobber and can carry a large wet fly behind it. Carry a few of these with you and use them if you encounter adverse stream conditions.

Convertible Stimulator

Hook: Size 6-16 long-shank
dry fly
Thread: 6/0 yellow
Tail: Deer hair
Body: Yellow poly yarn
Hackle: Cree
Wings: Deer hair

STRIKE INDICATOR

Have you ever had a trout strike your indicator? I have. Jerry Meck, Bob Sankey, Al Gretz, Terry Carlsen, and I try to get together to fish and reminisce about past great fishing trips we've shared. And we've had plenty of them, from Pennsylvania to Alaska. We are now all up in years, but that doesn't stop us from getting together.

Jerry consistently uses a bright orange-red strike indicator and Bob Sankey a fluorescent chartreuse one (the small, round ones pegged to the leader with a toothpick). In the two days we fished together I bet Jerry had ten trout strike his indicator; Bob had five. If those indicators had hooks, they would have caught fifteen more trout.

Several years ago I designed a pattern called the Strike Indicator that has fluorescent-orange poly wings, body, and tail with a parachute-style hackle. After a trout hit Jerry's indicator a tenth time, I had enough and tied on an orange Strike Indicator. Within seconds I landed a trout on the pattern. Two more trout hit it before we stopped fishing two hours later. That's three trout I never would have seen unless I used that fly. Other anglers must have had the same experience as me, because I've seen other strike indicator flies in my travels.

Strike Indicator

Hook:	Size 12-14 dry fly
Thread:	6/0 orange or chartreuse
Tail:	Orange or chartreuse poly yarn
Body:	Orange or chartreuse poly yarn
Hackle:	Dark brown
Wings:	White calf-body hair

LOOPED-LEADER DRY FLY (PATRIOT)

I developed looped-leader flies after thinking about an easy way to attach and remove a fly from my leader without knots. Make the loop large enough that you can attach it to a loop on your leader easily—even in the half-light before darkness. Even if you are not fishing the tandem, looped flies can be good options for you if you fish at or after dark. As long as you tie in the loop as shown below, it will be strong enough to hold any fish that you catch on the pattern.

TYING THE LOOPED-LEADER PATRIOT

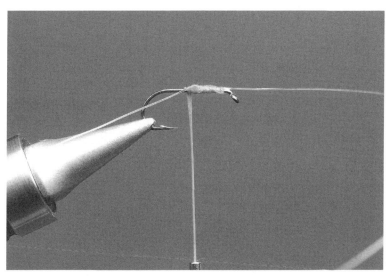

1. Tie in a 6-inch piece of 3X to 6X leader just behind the hook eye so that approximately 3 inches extends over the eye. Try to match the loop diameter with the diameter of the leader where you will place the looped fly. If your second piece of leader is 4X, and that's where you plan to place the looped dry fly, tie the loop with 4X leader. If you want to eventually take the looped fly off the leader, a heavier diameter leader like 3X is better.

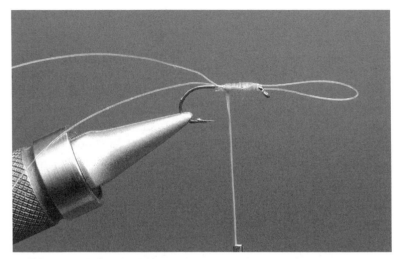

2. Take the end of the leader extending out over the eye and form a small loop in front of the hook eye one-quarter to one-inch long depending on your preference. Wind the tying thread over the ends of the leader about ten times and back to the hook bend so it's out of the way.

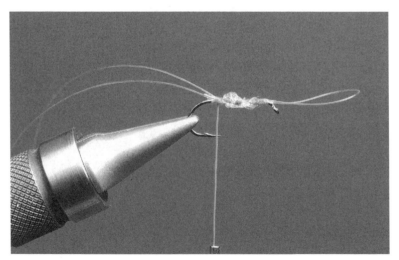

3. Make four half hitches with the two loose ends of the leader. Slip the hitch over the loop at the front and onto the hook. Space the half hitches so you don't form a lump.

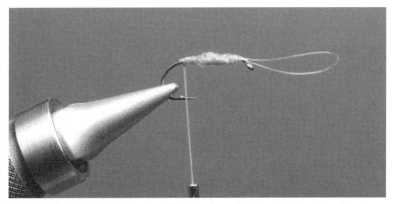

4. Cover the ends of the leader with tying thread back to the hook bend and cut the excess butt sections. Add head cement. Make plenty of wraps back to the hook bend and then back to the eye. Don't worry about crowding the eye—you'll never use it.

5. Tie in the white calf-body wing. Before wrapping thread in front of the wing, pull the wing up and out of the way of the leader loop. Make the loop shorter or longer than the length of the wings so the two are easier to separate. Wind the tying thread in front of the wings to make them stand erect. Continue tying the pattern as you normally would. When you complete the pattern make a series of half hitches over the loop and onto the shank. I apply plenty of head cement to the leader on the body and to the finished head, and sometimes even a drop or two of Super Glue.

6. The finished fly.

CHAPTER 9

▬▬▬▬▬▬▬

Subsurface Fly Patterns

Wet flies are fished under the surface and copy everything from aquatic insect nymphs and larvae to scuds and sowbugs to baitfish. Wet flies also copy sunken mayfly duns and spinners and caddisfly adults that have re-entered the water to lay eggs. For years most fly fishers thought all nymphs changed to duns at the surface, and that's where we fished most of our emerger patterns. More recently, many anglers have realized that many mayflies change from nymphs to duns at or near the bottom. Many of those old wet-fly patterns copied these mayflies moving to the surface and we didn't realize it. We did know that these wet flies caught fish. When my dry fly doesn't seem to produce, I'll often tug it underneath the surface and catch trout.

Wet-fly construction has changed dramatically in recent years. In the 1950s and 1960s, with a limited supply of fly-tying materials, most wet flies had wings made of barred feathers or quill sections from a mallard duck. Now many tiers use synthetic materials. Those classic wet-fly patterns like the Leadwing Coachman and Blue Dun still work, but many have almost vanished from the scene now that we have a wider array of materials available.

You have to limit your selection to a manageable few or you'll go crazy. Donald DuBois lists almost 6,000 patterns in his book *Fisherman's Handbook of Trout Flies* (1960), and wet flies make up most of these patterns. Can you imagine how many patterns a similar book would contain today? The following patterns are the ones that I carry all of the time and rely on the most. I use them when there is nothing hatching, and I can often use some of the imitative ones—such as the Pheasant Tail Nymph or Zebra Midge—to match the hatch.

When you see insects on the water and trout rising, then it's often a good idea to try and match the hatch—at least size, general color, and shape. And, if you're planning to fish new water, find out from locals the most effective patterns. In addition to these, I also carry nymphs for specific hatches on the streams that I fish the most.

Most of the wet flies included here have beads, which I think are one of the most significant changes in fly design in the past two decades. They make good flies great. Beads perform several functions. First, a bead helps sink the pattern more quickly. Before beads, tiers had to add weight to the body or lead shot to the leader to get the fly deeper. Now, a bead can often take the place of lead wraps and split-shot, though for heavier currents, tiers use a combination of weights. Beads are made from different material, and the material changes the rate at which they sink. The most popular bead colors are gold, brass, copper, nickel and black. The most effective colors for me are brass and copper. Beads also may represent the bubble many emerging nymphs have that might be a trigger for trout. I most often tie my beadhead patterns on a scud hook. If you don't tie flies, you can slide a bead onto your leader before you tie on the fly to make any pattern an instant beadhead.

These patterns work for me. Your list of flies might be totally different. But, constantly test new patterns and add those to your box that you feel work best. You can tie all of these wet flies with a looped leader.

BEADHEAD PHEASANT TAIL/TURKEY TAIL NYMPH

Many of the most successful subsurface patterns have several common ingredients. First, many have short, dark-brown tails and dark-brown bodies. Second, the body is often ribbed with fine gold or silver wire. Add a bead, and you have a wet fly that catches trout anywhere in the world: the Beadhead Pheasant Tail. This nymph consistently continues to be one of my best, wherever I fish. The Pheasant Tail represents many different mayfly nymphs in trout streams around the world. It copies *Baetis* and Sulphur/PMD mayfly nymphs found across the country, and many other insects with dark brownish-black to black bodies. For darker nymphs, I use turkey tail-feather fibers.

I most often fish the pattern 24 to 36 inches behind the dry fly, though conditions may warrant fishing it deeper or shallower. For instance, if a Sulphur hatch has or is appearing, then fish the Pheasant Tail shallower. In cold, deep water, fish the pattern deeper.

Pheasant Tail Nymph

Hook:	Size 12-20 curved shank
Bead:	Copper
Thread:	6/0 dark brown
Tail:	Pheasant-tail fibers
Body:	Pheasant-tail fibers ribbed with fine gold wire
Hackle:	Pheasant-tail fibers

The Flashback Beadhead Pheasant Tail is an effective variation of the Pheasant Tail that uses Flashabou as a wing case and a peacock-herl thorax.

ZEBRA MIDGE

Gary Hitterman of Casa Grande, Arizona, is one of the finest fly tiers I have ever met. He tied up a few Zebra Midge patterns (invented by Edward (Ted) Welling) for me when he heard I planned to fish the Colorado River at Lee's Ferry in northern Arizona. Frank Nofer from Philadelphia, Pennsylvania, accompanied me on the float downriver from Marble Canyon Dam. Frank, Chad Bayles, our guide, and I all fished size 16 Zebra Midges under size 12 dry flies. For more than two hours, one of us had a fish on the line.

I brought the Zebra Midge back East in 2000 and first used it on Opening Day on Pennsylvania's Bald Eagle Creek, a marginal stream because the planted trout either leave the stream, die, or swim to one of the cooler tributaries by July. That morning I had trouble finding a place to fish along the angler-littered shore. More than twenty anglers crowded around one pool that evidently had been stocked with trout. I was the only fool using flies. All the others used spinners, live bait, Power Bait, or salmon eggs.

The season began at 8 A.M. and not one of the bait and hardware anglers had much success for the first hour or two. Then I noticed a trout flash at the tail of the pool, and soon I saw a second fish turn and feed on something. I glanced in the direction of the two feeding trout, and I saw a few midges escape into the air. I quickly tied on a Zebra Midge under my dry fly and cast it toward the two flashing fish. Imagine fishing on a cold April day with twenty bait fishermen surrounding you, while you cast a fly to recently-stocked trout. The third drift through the tailout brought a strike and a twelve-inch rainbow. I heard murmurs from the other anglers circling the pool, and the whispers grew louder when I picked up a fifteen-inch brown trout in a few more casts.

When I landed the fifth trout, one guy bellowed: "Hey fella, there's another pool upstream a hundred yards." After a few minutes, I hiked upstream to the next pool, where I had similar success. I began to get a bit nervous with all of those anglers (who were as-of-yet fishless) talking.

Everywhere I've tested this pattern it works. On the Delaware River near Hancock, New York; on the Little Lehigh near Allentown,

Pennsylvania—the Zebra Midge has brought strikes when some of my other favorite patterns failed. If your favorite stream has midges (and chances are it does), try the Zebra Midge.

I usually fish the Zebra Midge from two to five feet behind a Patriot. In heavy, cold water—I go deeper. I've noticed that depth really matters with this fly, like most patterns, and if I don't get strikes with it at one depth, I often will at a different depth. Without any extra weight, the streamline design and bead quickly take the fly deep.

Even a beginner can tie one quickly. The normal tie is a black body formed with tying thread, ribbed with fine silver wire, and a brass bead, but I tie some with dark brown or olive bodies, fine gold ribbing, and a copper bead and also have been successful with an assortment of other colors.

Zebra Midge

Hook:	Size 16-20 curved shank
Bead:	Brass (black body) or copper (brown and olive body)
Thread:	6/0 (not prewaxed) black, brown, or olive
Body:	Tying thread
Ribbing:	Fine silver (black body) or copper wire (brown and olive body)

ALMOST

When I arrived at the Little Juniata, at least twenty trout rose through a fast run in front of me. Curious about what was causing these fish to feed so heavily, I placed my small hand seine just under the surface and collected hundreds of small, pencil-point-thin midge larvae. They all had prominent ribbing on their bodies. After pondering for a moment, I blurted out to myself that these midges could be copied with a size 18 plain hook with fine gold ribbing. I went home and tied some. I put a brass bead on a size 18 scud hook, and wrapped the gold wire around itself at the bend and then ribbed the hook up to the bead. I added a drop of glue at the bend and the bead and let the pattern sit for a few minutes before I cut the excess wire. I called the pattern Almost because it's almost a bare hook. I've caught hundreds of trout with it; often when other patterns failed.

Paul Weamer, author of *Fly Fishing Guide to the Upper Delaware River* (Stackpole Books, 2007) and master fly tier, came fishing with me one morning and saw how effective the Almost can be. Nothing seemed to work, until I tried the Almost. That fly caught five heavy trout before we quit—two of the trout were large. Paul immediately went home and tied up a dozen.

Almost

Hook: Size 16-20 curved
          shank
Bead: Copper
Rib: Fine gold wire covered
          by head cement

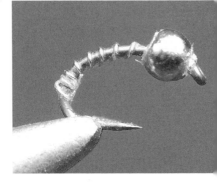

The Brassie is another wire-body fly that, tied with different colors of wire, can imitate a wide range of midges.

BEADHEAD OLIVE CADDIS

By mid-afternoon, I had little success to show for two hours of fishing with a Pheasant Tail. Then, I felt some weight on the line—what I thought was a sizable trout—that wasn't coming in easily. Finally, I saw what I caught, and it wasn't a fish. I had hooked a clump of submerged willow tree roots. As I untangled my fly from the mess, I noted lots of olive caddis larvae attached to the roots. I placed one in a vial, took it home, and tied several simple patterns to copy it. The one I liked best had a bead and olive body ribbed with gold wire.

The Beadhead Olive Caddis has often saved me from getting skunked. In 2005 on lower Bald Eagle Creek I had fished a July morning for two hours without one trout. I finally spotted a few dark olive caddis on the surface and switched to a Beadhead Olive Caddis. On each of the first ten casts, I caught trout—ten for ten. I quit, because I didn't want to break my streak. Besides, I planned to bring my son, Bryan, back to the same spot the next day, and I wanted him to have the same success.

I fish the Olive Caddis on a dead drift usually 24 to 36 inches behind the indicator fly, and sometimes go 36 to 60 inches. I tie several shades of olive for this pattern, and it works especially well during the summer on the waters that I fish.

Beadhead Olive Caddis

Hook: Size 12-16 curved shank
Bead: Copper
Thread: 6/0 olive
Body: Dark-olive opossum fur ribbed with fine gold wire

BEADHEAD TAN CADDIS

I first got acquainted with the Beadhead Tan Caddis on the Ruby River in southwestern Montana. For every trout I caught, my son, Bryan, caught five. It was humiliating. I pleaded with him to give me one of his flies. That evening we saw a heavy Tan Caddis hatch, and I realized why the pattern worked so well earlier that day.

I'll never forget that second day I used this fly if I live to be a hundred. Bryan, Ken Rictor, Lynn Rotz, Jerry Armstrong, and I headed to the upper end of the East Fork Ruby River, guided by Jake and Donna McDonald. The SUV towed a trailer with seven horses and traveled slowly up a deeply rutted road. We finally parked in an overgrown field and unloaded the horses, our transportation for the next ten miles.

I mounted my horse clumsily and slowly. I never rode a horse before and I was fearful. To make matters worse, I had undergone a hemorrhoid operation a few months before, and I was still in excruciating pain. Every jolt on the horse brought agony.

The horses followed each other, and I was in the rear of the pack. We traveled on a steep trail that at points was only a few feet wide. To the right and left, the terrain dropped at least two hundred feet. If these horses lost their balance or spooked, we'd be killed. I was so scared, on some parts of the trail, I just closed my eyes.

When we finally arrived at our destination my rear hurt too much to fish seriously. Plus, I couldn't stop thinking that we'd have to get back on the horses when we were done fishing. As distracted as I was I managed to land six trout on a Beadhead Tan Caddis. Bryan, Ken, and Lynn caught even more.

Beadhead Tan Caddis

Hook: Size 12-16 curved shank
Thread: 6/0 tan
Bead: Copper
Body: Tan opossum fur ribbed with fine gold wire

On the trip back to the car, we hit a thunderstorm and had no place to hide in the wide-open alpine fields, so we just kept riding. Lightning spewed across the open, treeless mountaintop. Bryan yelled as each bolt struck nearby. Some seemed to be within a half mile of us. We kept riding through a constant, heavy rain. I kept my eyes closed almost the entire trip back to the van. Finally, someone yelled that they saw the car. I guarantee that's the last horse ride I'll ever take—even if we did have good fishing with the Beadhead Tan Caddis.

So, that's my memory of the fly pattern. Since then, it has worked well for me in the East throughout the year, but especially in the evening from June through August as an imitation of the prevalent *Symphitopsyche* (formerly called *Hydropsyche*) species.

BEADHEAD GLO BUGS

For years I shunned Glo Bugs because they represented fish eggs, until Bruce Matolyak showed me how this pattern consistently catches trout when no other pattern does. After seeing Bruce catch a half-dozen trout while I caught none, I recanted, tried the Glo Bug, and haven't been without a good supply since.

I have always had the most success fishing the fly near the bottom. However, conventionally tied Glo Bugs don't sink quickly enough. I add a bead and shove five or six turns of .010-inch-diameter lead wire into the large hole. Not only does the bead help sink the pattern more quickly, it looks like an egg yolk.

There are many different ways to tie Glo Bugs, so I'll explain how I do it. Tie two 2-inch strips of Glo Bug yarn midshank on top of the hook and pull tight. After you make three or four tight turns with the tying thread around the material and the shank, make about twelve turns around the base of the material like you would for a parachute post. Cut the two strands closest to the hook eye at an upward angle and the two strands closest to the bend at a downward angle. I carry scissors with me and like to finish trimming the fly onstream.

Blueberry

I used to be convinced cream was the best Glo Bug color. That color consistently caught fish throughout the year. Recently I dyed some yarn Rit evening-blue. I handed Ed Sato one of these blue Glo Bugs when he fished with me. As the blue Glo Bug sank to the bottom, five trout surrounded the fly, and finally one hit. This action continued for hours. After Ed and I quit fishing, I cut the fly from his leader, and told him it was experimental and I didn't want word to get out. Ed looked at me, his mouth agape with disbelief.

In 1973 Ginetz and Larkin reported in "Colors of Food Items by Rainbow Trout" that hatchery-raised rainbows often preferred blue eggs over other colors. The scientists placed dyed rainbow trout eggs in troughs (in natural light) and the trout preferred the following colors (in order of preference): blue, red, black, orange, yellow, and green. In another experiment, the two scientists used four egg colors (blue, red, black, and yellow) and matched the background with each color. For example, they used a blue background when they fed the trout blue eggs and a red background when they fed them red eggs. In this latter experiment, trout ate the blue eggs more often than any other color.

There's no blue egg in nature, and I have no clue why blue works so well. Because of that article, I tied the Patriot with a blue body. That dry fly has performed well for me for more than 15 years. The Blueberry has caught trout when no other pattern has.

One day I experimented with several wet flies, including the Blueberry. I decided to cast each one hundred times and then count how many trout struck each pattern. I first recorded the Beadhead Emerger, then the Cream Glo Bug, and the Zebra Midge. I fished all of these on a warm July afternoon under bright sunny skies on a private stream loaded with trout. In one hundred casts the Zebra Midge caught five trout, the Beadhead Emerger six, and the cream Glo Bug seven. Then I tied on the Blueberry. On each cast five to ten trout swirled around the pattern before one finally hit. This action occurred on each of the first ten casts and reminded me of a drug trial where the drug was so superior they ended the trial early. After the tenth cast, I quit the experiment.

One day in late July, Diane and Jim Ryan and Jim's brother Bill fished together. Both Jim and Diane recently retired for Penn State University so they had more time to fish, hunt, and enjoy their new home in Laporte, Pennsylvania. Before the trip that day I had tied up a dozen Blueberries so we'd have enough. I didn't estimate correctly: We ran out by early evening. Jim swears that he caught the same 18-inch trout three times that day on that pattern.

To get the right color for the Blueberry, dye white or cream Glo Bug yarn with Rit evening-blue dye. Keep checking the color of the yarn until it's medium blue. To fix the dye, take a piece out and run cold water over it.

The Blueberry has caught trout everywhere I've used it: from the Colorado River at Lees Ferry, to the lagoons at Dead Horse State Park near Cottonwood, Arizona, to Brodhead Creek in northeastern Pennsylvania.

Blueberry

Hook:	Size 12-16 curved shank
Bead:	Brass
Thread:	6/0 bright orange-red
Body:	Two strands of Glo Bug Yarn dyed evening blue (Rit dye)

Bicolor

Ginetz and Larkin also tested how trout react to two colors at the same time. They found that when yellow and black dyed salmon eggs were presented to the fish, trout fed more actively. As a result of that experiment, I tied up several Glo Bugs half yellow and half black.

Christopher Budd first used these Glo bugs. I worked with 15-year-old Christopher on his casting one day and handed him one of these yellow-and-black eggs to try. In the next three hours he

In high, off-color water, this brown ate a Bicolor Glo Bug tied to the bend of a Patriot.

landed fifteen trout on the pattern. On many occasions, when nothing else worked, I have tied on a Bicolor Glo Bug and it has caught trout. After writing about the pattern in *Mid Atlantic Fly Fishing Guide,* several anglers contacted me to tell me the success they had with the fly.

Bicolor Glo Bug

Hook:	Size 12-16 curved shank
Bead:	Copper
Thread:	6/0 yellow
Body:	One yellow and one black piece of Glo Bug Yarn

The Grape

In tests reported in *Western Outdoors* in "What They See," I read that violet penetrated the deepest in water. As a result of that article I tied a Glo Bug that I had dyed violet and called it the Grape.

ORANGE CADDIS LARVA

Ben Rooke sat behind me and kibitzed about my choice of patterns, my casting ability, and just about anything else he felt I was doing incorrectly.

"Here, try this one," Ben urged, as he handed me an odd orange-bodied wet fly.

"I have plenty of patterns," I replied. Ben finally convinced me to try the ugly orange fly he called a "killer" pattern. I tied on the size 12 Orange Caddis. After a few casts, the Patriot sank and I set the hook. In less than a minute a huge rainbow, well over 20 inches long, had broken my 6X fluorocarbon tippet. I looked toward Ben, and without hesitating, he handed me another. On the third cast, the Patriot sank as another heavy rainbow hit the fly. I fought this fish for more than five minutes before it, too, broke the fine tippet.

"Why don't you use a heavier tippet?" Ben asked, after I lost the fish.

I tore off the 6X tippet and replaced it with 5X, and Ben tied on a third Orange Caddis pattern.

I broke off several more behemoths before I quit, and I went home that evening and tied two dozen of them.

Orange Caddis Larva

Hook:	Size 12-16 curved shank
Thread:	6/0 orange
Body:	Bright orange wool or other yarn ribbed with fine gold wire
Collar:	Several turns of dark dun hackle

You might have come across a bright orange caddis larva that is a member of the genus of the Little Black Caddis (*Chimarra atterima*) common in many trout streams in early spring. If your stream holds this early spring caddis hatch, then this orange-bodied larva pattern should be a killer. If you use the pattern in the fall, try a size 16 or 18. If you fish the fly just before the adult emerges in early spring, try a size 12 or 14. I weight the hook before I tie the fly so that I can fish the pattern deep.

GREEN WEENIE

It's been sixteen years since I first saw an angler use the Green Weenie. When I began researching *Pennsylvania Trout Streams and Their Hatches,* Russ Mowry invited me to fish Loyalhanna Creek about forty miles east of downtown Pittsburgh. Russ, Ken Igo, and Tim Shaffer took me to the delayed-harvest section of the stream for an afternoon of late-March fishing. Five other anglers fished the same pool as us. But soon those other five anglers watched in disbelief at what my three friends did. In two hours of fishing Russ, Tim, and Ken caught more than twenty-five trout while not one of the other five anglers had even a strike. Why did these three do well and the others have nothing to show for their casting effort? Two words: Green Weenie.

Barry Staats, owner of the Sporting Gentleman Orvis shop in Media, Pennsylvania, sells thousands of Green Weenies each year. He sells so many of these simply tied, odd-colored patterns because the fly often works when no other pattern does. It has saved the day for me on the Salt River in Arizona, on the McKenzie River in central Oregon, on a lake at Isaac's Ranch in central Washington, and even on Irondequoit Creek, a small stream near Rochester, New York. On these and dozens of other rivers across the United States, the Green Weenie has caught trout when no other pattern did.

I'll never ever forget that day on Isaac's Ranch in central Washington. George Cook, one of the finest fly casters in the world, was our host. George is the consummate fishing guide and was passing out patterns to try and find something that worked for us. When he handed me the fourth pattern, I furtively placed it in my fly box, and instead I tied on a Green Weenie. On the first cast I landed a heavy rainbow. George nodded, as if saying that at last the pattern he had handed me did the trick. Two more casts, and I caught another heavy rainbow. Wow! This was fun. George again nodded. I had difficulty extricating the fly from the third heavy rainbow, and George came over to help out. I felt like Sammy Sosa after the umpires found cork in his bat. The secret was out. When George finally dislodged the Green Weenie from the fish, he looked up at me and asked what the devil that fly was. I told him it was a Green Weenie, he asked me for a couple, and then handed them to the two other anglers fishing nearby.

You may laugh when you first see the Green Weenie, but over the years I've realized that bright green fly imitates everything from inchworms to caddis larvae to damselfly nymphs.

Green Weenie

Hook: Size 10-12 Mustad 9672
Thread: 6/0 chartreuse
Body: 15 wraps of .010-inch-diameter lead. Take a 5-inch piece of small or medium chartreuse chenille and form a small loop that extends over the hook bend, tie the loop down, and then wrap the chenille around the hook shank to the eye.

HARTMAN'S BROWN CADDIS EMERGER

I've learned much from fishing with Ed Hartt—or, more precisely, watching him fish. One day I watched Ed fish a new fly he called the Brown Caddis Emerger, developed by Craig Hartman of Altoona, Pennsylvania. In an hour, he landed more than a dozen trout, and that day was not a fluke. The Brown Caddis Emerger has caught trout for me in all parts of the United States and under all types of water conditions. It looks a lot like the Pheasant Tail but has a dubbed thorax.

Hartman's Brown Caddis Emerger

Hook:	Size 12-20 curved shank
Bead:	Copper
Thread:	6/0 dark brown
Tail:	Pheasant-tail fibers
Body:	Pheasant-tail fibers ribbed with gold wire
Thorax:	Dark olive Squirrel Brite

BEADHEAD WOOLLY BUGGER

The Beadhead Woolly Bugger has saved the day for me on several fishing trips. One trip to the Little Colorado in northcentral Arizona would have been a complete disaster without it. The waters ran high, and Craig Josephson and I seemed doomed. For an entire morning we fished various flies without a strike. Desperate, I tied on a Beadhead Woolly Bugger. It couldn't have been more than three casts before I caught my first rainbow. After several more casts, a three-pound brown trout struck. I hurriedly ran down to where Craig fished.

"Tear off that fly," I told him. "Try this one."

Within minutes, Craig began catching trout, and this action continued all afternoon until the two patterns were tattered beyond recognition. One fly completely turned around the trip. At dinner, the river keeper for the X Diamond Ranch said that we were the first to do well on the river in four days. I'm certain we would have continued to do poorly had we not changed flies.

You can fish the Woolly Bugger alone or with another fly. It's deadly when fished with another streamer, with a nymph trailed off the bend, or fished under a large, buoyant dry. I like to fish the Bugger deep, letting it swing, and often impart motion to the fly. In high water trout seem to hit this pattern with a vengeance, perhaps because it represents a wide range of foods that get swept into the currents after high water, such as hellgrammites, cranefly larvae, large nymphs, baitfish, and crayfish.

If you fish this pattern under a dry fly, tie it on a fairly small hook. A lot of people fish large Woolly Buggers and overlook small versions of this fly. Normally, I tie the Woolly Bugger on a size 10, extra-long streamer hook. I tie Woolly Buggers fished under a dry on size 14-16, 2X-long hooks weighted with ten wraps of .005- or .010-inch-diameter lead.

Beadhead Woolly Bugger

Hook: Size 6-12 Mustad 9672
Thread: Black
Bead: Copper
Tail: Six pieces of black marabou and six pieces of Flashabou
Body: Small or medium olive chenille, ribbed with gold wire and palmered with a black saddle hackle

ROOKE'S MINNOW

When Ben Rooke first showed me the pattern, I thought it was a hoax and laughed. Ben swore me to secrecy but later said it was okay to write about it.

The body of the fly is a piece of a tan chamois wrapped around the hook with the smoother side facing up, extended about the length of the hook shank beyond the bend. Rooke palmers a badger hackle over the chamois body. Rooke adds two or three lead shot to his leader 12 to 18 inches above the fly. Instead of split-shot, I weight the fly. You can fish this fly behind a large dry or fish it with another streamer like the Woolly Bugger.

Maybe trout take it for a sculpin or crayfish. In my fifty-plus years of fly fishing I have never seen trout take a fly as aggressively as Rooke's Minnow.

Rooke's Minnow

Hook:	Size 12 Mustad 9672
Thread:	6/0 tan
Bead:	Copper
Tail:	Flashabou or Krystal Flash
Body:	Tan chamois palmered with a badger saddle hackle

CHAPTER 10

Final Casts

In the Introduction, I described my exciting fishing trip with guide Dave Trimble on the Colorado River at Lee's Ferry. That day was one of the most eventful of my fishing career. Dave caught his largest trout ever on the river, and I was coaching him. Dave did everything right, and he was rewarded with a trophy trout.

What did he do correctly? First, he used the tandem. Not only is this rig the preferred setup on the lower Colorado, it's my technique of choice on most streams and rivers I fish. Dave used a highly visible dry fly as his lead fly and selected a good fly for his subsurface pattern, the Blueberry. I'm confident none of the fish on the river saw that pattern before, and I think that matters. Several anglers who drifted past us on the river that day asked what we were catching our trout on. When I showed them the Blueberry, they admitted it was first time they had seen the fly.

To land that fish, Dave used strong and fine leaders, which were fluorocarbon. But leader strength is no better than the knots you use to connect them, and Dave's knots held. Dave fished the Blueberry on the bottom, just where those heavy rainbows cruised. Everything came together: the right rig, fly, depth, and presentation.

I first wrote about using the tandem in *Patterns, Hatches, Tactics and Trout* in 1995. I was excited about the prospects of using this system in the East and I wanted to spread the word. Just a few weeks after the book came out, I received a letter from Pete Ryan, who lives in northcentral Pennsylvania. As soon as Pete bought my book, he tested the tandem with some of the patterns that I suggested and sent me the following letter.

I'm writing to share a couple fishing experiences I had this past week! I received your new book a week ago Thursday and read most of it that afternoon and evening. I was, of course, interested in the tandem—Patriot and Green Weenie—and while watching football games on Sunday, I tied a dozen Patriots and weighted Green Weenies. I intended to fish Labor Day morning on the no-kill stretch of the Genesee River east of Wellsville, New York. . . . I left my house determined to try the tandem and took only those flies plus a box of Tricos and midges—just in case.

I arrived in the parking area at 9:30 only to meet Bryan Kehoe, one of my fishing buddies, leaving the stream. He was disgusted—having fished for three hours and no trout. I explained to him what I intended to do and showed him the two flies. He laughed and tried to talk me into going to the Oswayo, a Pennsylvania stream a few miles away, but I was determined to give the tandem a chance. So as Bryan watched from his car, I caught two nice browns on my first five casts in the first run! He yelled an obscenity at me as he drove away!

I quit fishing at 12:30 after an additional twelve trout—all on the Green Weenie. Not bad, fourteen trout in three hours on a heavily fished, no-kill stream with no surface activity, no hatches, and drought conditions. I even got home in time to mow my lawn, with a smile on my face!

Last Wednesday night, Stew Dickerson, with whom you fished the Oswayo a few years back, gave me a call and said he had done really well fishing Tricos and ants on the Genesee in Scio, New York, about 6 miles downstream from Wellsville. Stew knows I love fishing small flies on fine tippets to rising fish, so of course I jumped at the chance. The next morning the stream, as expected, was extremely low, but there were five deep runs in the half-mile stretch that Stew promised held fish. Tricos were dancing in the air when we hit the stream at 8 A.M. Stew caught two trout on an ant, and I could only manage a few smallmouth bass fishing a midge in the first run. We worked our way upstream fishing ants, beetles, midges, and Trico spinners, and by 10 A.M. I managed to catch two trout and Stew also had a few more.

Stew started to apologize for our lack of success after his glowing promise of great fishing. I told Stew to relax—I was about to give the tandem another try! Three casts into that run that I had pounded for twenty-five minutes produced two trout. In five minutes I had five trout. Stew begged a Patriot and Green Weenie off me, and we proceeded to work our way back downstream to the car. Between us, we caught thirty-one trout in the next two hours, all on the Green Weenie, except for one 17 1/2-inch brown that blasted my Patriot as it danced in a riffle at the head of a deep run.

I have also fished the tandem on the Big Horn, but never thought to bring it home. Just want to thank you for sharing your expertise with those of us who aren't as fortunate to fish as often as you are able. My only concern is that the tandem may take the excitement and pleasure out of fooling fish—but I doubt it.

INDEX